Bill Barnes
4/13/05

MORE ADVANCE PRAISE FOR

DOING BUSINESS BY THE GOOD BOOK:

* * *

"Dave shows in this book that you can follow the Golden Rule and still run a successful company. His words, as well as his actions, are an inspiration to all business leaders."

–Robert L. Bagby, Chairman and CEO, A.G. Edwards, Inc.

"*Doing Business by the Good Book* should be required reading by every CEO in America."

–C. Britt Beemer, Chairman and CEO, America's Research Group

"David Steward is a successful businessman and an outstanding civic leader. His life should serve as an example that hard work and perseverance can overcome all obstacles."

–Bob Holden, Governor of Missouri

"David Steward is a deeply religious man who has been successful in business. He is now sharing his vision of life and ethics in business. The reader will come away a better person."

–William H. Danforth, Chancellor Emeritus, Washington University in St. Louis

"David Steward's deep faith has enabled him to lead and educate others in working and living at the highest possible levels. What enormous benefit he brings to the world of business–and to all our lives."

–Alan Schonberg, Founder and Chairman Emeritus, Management Recruiters International

"David Steward hits the nail on the head. This book demonstrates how his great business success is closely related to his profound faith."

–George H. Walker, U.S. Ambassador to Hungary

"Personal honesty and integrity may be more important than ever to growing a business and building strong customer relationships. Steward's clear, practical discussion of ethical issues offers lessons any business person will find useful."

–Andrew C. Taylor, Chairman and CEO, Enterprise Rent-A-Car

"Today, American businesses are being challenged to create the right 'Tone at the Top' in order to manage successfully through difficult times. Dave Steward takes the issue squarely on, by making a timely and eloquent case that the principles upon which our faith tells us to live our personal lives also apply to our business activities."

–Douglas H. Yaeger, Chairman of the Board, President and CEO, The Laclede Group, Inc.

"WOW. This book contains truly substantive life lessons. No matter how large or small your enterprise, these fifty-two philosophies will speak to your soul."

–Mayor Michael Coleman, Columbus, Ohio

"I found *Doing Business by the Good Book* very stimulating and very enlightening. Many talk about the separation of church and state or business, but if we follow the guidelines as set down in the Bible, we will always be on track."

–Robert A. Reynolds, Chairman, President and CEO, Graybar Electric Company, Inc.

"I enjoyed the book and felt blessed by having read it. It will certainly help me to be more consistent in applying the first ServiceMaster corporate objective, 'To honor God in all we do.' "

–Michael M. Isakson, President and CEO, ServiceMaster Clean and Furniture Medic

"I have worked side by side with Dave since July 1990 when we first opened the doors to World Wide Technology, Inc. His unwavering commitment to stand behind his word in good times and in bad and always do what is right has been the foundation of our thirteen year relationship and this business."

–Jim Kavanagh, CEO, World Wide Technology Holding, Inc.

"We learn from David Steward the importance of setting our affections on things above, not on things on the earth–of serving Christ as the surest foundation for building our personal and professional lives."

–Ronald Q. Williams, Assistant Regional Administrator, Federal Technology Service,
U.S. General Services Administration

"David Steward, by using real-life examples of results based on his commitment to God, brings new life and meaning to business through the Good Book."

–Dr. Richard S. Meyers, President of Webster University

"David Steward weaves lessons from the Bible with his own faith-filled and inspiring life story to demonstrate how morality, spirituality and service to others are not only compatible with true success, but absolutely necessary to it."

–Missouri Attorney General Jay Nixon

"The ethical and moral source for doing business as outlined in this book is exactly what American business needs at this time."

–Richard Vehige, President, Catholic Charities Archdiocese of St. Louis, MO

"Concepts like respect, love-in-action, fairness, care, and concern for the well-being of his employees and customers are the priorities of Dave Steward's life. Here is a book that both teaches and inspires."

–Ann Brookshire Sherer, Resident Bishop, Missouri Conference, The United Methodist Church

"David Steward has demonstrated how to apply Biblical principles and Christian ethics on a daily basis while doing business with integrity."

–Reverend Jeremiah A. Wright, Jr., Senior Pastor, Trinity United Church of Christ, Chicago, IL

"Dave Steward's book proves that when one lives a moral life, both prosperity and fulfillment follow. This is a good read for anyone in business."

–Patrick Mulcahy, CEO Energizer Holdings, Inc.

"In this book, Dave Steward has translated the noblest values of life into practical work day applications. In doing so, David has not only demonstrated that these values work in business, but that they can actually be the catalyst for growth."

–Gary Dollar, President and CEO, The United Way of Greater St. Louis, MO

"This book is filled with excellent and timely advice for both the novice and experienced businessperson. I thoroughly enjoyed reading it."

–Bob LaMonte, President and founder, Professional Sports Representation, Inc.

"This book delivers the blueprint for true success, built on the truth that will set you free!"

–*Tim Templeton, author of* The Referral of a Lifetime

"It's a powerful experience to witness someone living his faith, and through *Doing Business by the Good Book*, David offers insight for others to do the same."

–*Arnold Donald, Chairman and CEO of Merisant Company*

"The leadership principles outlined in this book and exemplified by David Steward are timeless. They will bless everyone who reads and practices them."

–*Robert Clark, CEO, Clayco Construction Company*

"This is an inspirational book for those who value morality in business. The wisdom of the Bible teaches that by doing good, you will ultimately do well."

–*Lillian Vernon, Founding Chairman, Lillian Vernon Corporation*

"All who read this book will be blessed and will in turn bless others."

–*Ralph W. Clermont, Managing Partner, KPMG LLP*

"*Doing Business by the Good Book* is essential reading for anyone intent on succeeding in business the right way."

–*Thurmond B. Woodward, Chief Ethics Officer and Vice President of Global Diversity, Dell, Inc.*

"David Steward is a man of integrity. His values-based approach to business and life has made him a success at both."

–*Joseph J. Anderson, Vice President, Quality Management and Supplier Diversity, Verizon Communications*

"David Steward's book is a remarkable testimony of the power of love–in all of our thoughts and all that we attempt to do."

–*Dr. Henry Givens Jr., President, Harris-Stowe State College*

Doing Business by the Good Book

DOING BUSINESS BY THE GOOD BOOK

52 Lessons on Success Straight from the Bible

DAVID L. STEWARD
WITH ROBERT L. SHOOK

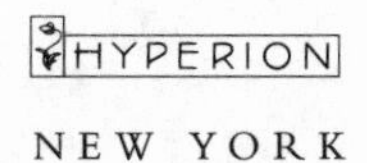

NEW YORK

To Thelma, who is the center of my life.

With much love, Dave

For information address: Hyperion, 77 West 66th Street, New York, New York 10023-6298.

Library of Congress Cataloging-in-Publication Data

Steward, David.

Doing business by the Good Book : fifty-two lessons on success straight from the Bible / David Steward with Robert L. Shook.–1st ed.

p. cm.

ISBN 1-4013-0062-6

1. Business–Religious aspects. 2. Business–Biblical teaching. 3. Business ethics. 4. Success in business. I. Shook, Robert L., 1938– II. Title.

HF5388.S74 2004

658–dc21

2003047890

Hyperion books are available at special quantity discounts to use as premiums or for special programs, including corporate training. For details contact Michael Rentas, Manager, Inventory and Premium Sales, Hyperion, 77 West 66th Street, 11th floor, New York, New York 10023, or call 212-456-0133.

FIRST EDITION

10 9 8 7 6 5 4 3 2

— ACKNOWLEDGMENTS —

I have been blessed to have many people make valuable contributions to this book. First and foremost, my wife, Thelma, who helped to select appropriate scripture for every chapter. She is a fountain of knowledge and wisdom on the Word of God. She was my inspiration throughout the writing of this book. I thank God every day for giving me Thelma, my lifetime partner and soul mate.

I am blessed to have Bob Shook as my collaborator on this book. I admire his perseverance, work ethic, and passion. During the past year, we formed an endearing friendship, one that we both cherish. Hence, this book represents the first of several collaborations as well as the beginning of a lifelong relationship. I am indebted to his wife, Elinor, for having shared Bob's time with me so he could devote long hours on this book so we could meet our publishing deadline.

I am very grateful to the members of our Business by the Book Sunday school class that meets every Sunday morning at the Union Memorial United Methodist Church. The class was the catalyst that inspired the idea for this book. I am thankful to Ray Burrows and Art Kimbrough, who initiated this project. And it was Ray who served as a liaison between Bob and me in the beginning.

Ray, along with Art Kimbrough, Chris Kiersch, Ken Jones, David Nicklaus, and Nick Barris are members of our marketing team, a committee dedicated to assure wide distribution so the book can accomplish our mission to "spread the Word." Ray, Art, Chris, Ken, and David, along with Thelma, were our biggest cheerleaders from start to finish. Any success that this book enjoys will be a direct result of their combined talents and commitment.

I am grateful to Patti DeSoto Carr, my executive assistant, who took on additional responsibilities along with her normal workload to schedule and coordinate interviews between Bob and me so we could work long-distance between St. Louis and Columbus, Ohio. Her assistance made an otherwise difficult task seem effortless. Bob joins me in acknowledging Patti for her outstanding work.

A special thank you goes to my good friend George H. "Bert" Walker for introducing our manuscript to President George H. W. Bush, who graciously wrote the foreword to this book.

We thank Debbie Watts, who transcribed hundreds of hours of recorded interviews; and Maggie Abel, Bob's able assistant, who helped to prepare the manuscript. Debbie and Maggie excel in their work.

Bob and I are grateful to have Al Zuckerman, founder and president of Writers House, represent us as our agent. We acknowledge Al as a man of high integrity, talent, and creativity. Thank you, Al, for taking us to Hyperion, the perfect publisher for this book. Last, but by no means least, we were blessed to have a sensational editor, Mary Ellen O'Neill. (MEO–you instantaneously won our hearts at that very first meeting in Hyperion's conference room.) We marvel at Mary Ellen's enthusiasm and skill–her commitment and support are greatly appreciated.

May God bless all of these outstanding people.

A Special Acknowledgment

No single person builds a successful organization. I am forever grateful to the men and women who work at WWT; without them, this company would not exist nor would this book have been written. While it is not possible to list the individual names of the five-hundred-plus members of the WWT family, I would be remiss if I didn't acknowledge Jim Kavanaugh, who helped start WWT back in 1990, along with Joe Koenig and Tom Strunk, who joined us a few years later. Our shared commitment to excellence has evolved into a unique brand of leadership. Working as a team for many years, we have developed a strong bond that has spawned a special relationship among us rarely exhibited in the workplace. May God continue to richly bless these individuals and the WWT family.

CONTENTS

FOREWORD

David Steward has come up with an idea that betters the way we live and work. The idea that he embodies is not actually new–it is a 2000-year-old philosophy that makes as much sense today as it did back then.

In 1990, when Dave Steward founded his St. Louis–based World Wide Technology, his mission was to build a successful company based on teachings he had learned from the Bible. He believes individual values should not be separated from corporate values, and he adheres to the philosophy that good ethics is good business. He contends that the same qualities of integrity, trust, commitment, and loyalty that we expect from our friends and family are also appropriate in the workplace.

David's mission is to make a positive difference in other people's lives, to produce a better quality of life for those he touches–his employees, as well as his vendors and customers. "We're here to serve each other," he says. "As CEO, my first priority is to serve my employees. Properly done, this attitude will permeate my organization and carry over to those we do business with–and we will be successful."

David Steward has been successful, building a billion-dollar company identified by *Black Enterprise* as the largest African-American–owned company in 2000. His story of success epitomizes the American Dream, and his example is an inspiration to us all.

–GEORGE H. W. BUSH

INTRODUCTION

When I founded World Wide Technology, Inc., in 1990, I wanted to run a company based on the teachings of the Bible. Starting on a shoestring and personally signing to borrow the much-needed capital made this a high-risk venture, and I was well aware of the high failure rate of highly leveraged start-up companies. Even after nearly ten years of working in sales for three established Fortune 500 companies, as an entrepreneur I was a novice and as green as they come. Despite that, I was certain I would ultimately succeed. My confidence wasn't based on a wealth of business acumen or a string of successes under my belt. I felt this way due to my unshakable faith in God. Having this faith, I believed with all my heart and soul that he would see me through.

At the time, many people thought that as an African-American, I didn't belong in the world of high technology. They resented my ambition and said I was in way over my head. This attitude wasn't limited to the white community; some of my most outspoken critics were in the African-American community.

I grew up in Clinton, Missouri, a small town about 250 miles southwest of St. Louis. As a teenager, I lived through the turbulent, racially tense sixties. Looking back to my boyhood, I vividly remember segregation–separate schools, sitting in the balcony at the movie theater, being barred from the public swimming pool, the for-whites-only Wiley's Restaurant, and so on. The degradation African-Americans endured in those days seemed to occur in a different lifetime compared to when I launched my company three decades later. Nonetheless, there were still people who didn't relish an African-American stepping on their turf. Still, so many positive things had happened regarding race in America since my youth, and there was no way I was going to harbor negative feelings toward my detractors. When I was a small boy, my mother warned me against becoming bitter and resentful. "David, those feelings are self-destructive and a waste of time," she cautioned me, always citing scripture to support her comment.

I have been blessed to have a wonderful family–nurturing parents and grandparents who enriched my life with wholesome values. These hardworking, churchgoing folks showered me with love and introduced me to the Word of God. Although they had few material possessions, they diligently taught me what was really important–by example. Consequently, I feel as if I inherited considerable wealth from them. What's more, God blessed me with an exceptional life partner, my wife, Thelma. Thelma has been enormously supportive, and her unyielding commitment to stand by me through thick and thin has been a true inspiration. Her faith in the vision God has given me is a great source of motivation.

Thelma demonstrates her faith in God by believing in me. Bear in mind, she has no role in my business but she *knows* it will succeed. I have an undying need to make a difference in other people's lives–and knowing Thelma recognizes this inspires me to succeed because I don't want to disappoint her, our children, David and Kim, or my extended family, the men and women who work at World Wide Technology.

Looking back to 1990 and the many obstacles we had to overcome, some people say we succeeded against all odds. "It was nothing short of a miracle," I've been told. I concur, but then when God is on your side, miracles happen. And what happened to us can happen to you. On what grounds do I make this statement? Because the Word tells us so. Countless citations in the Bible tell us we will be rewarded for adhering to the Word of God. Throughout this book, I refer to scripture to illustrate how this works. If you believe in the Bible as I do, you will share my belief that good things happen to those who have faith. In Deuteronomy 7:12–13, it is written: "If you heed these ordinances, by diligently observing them, the LORD your God will maintain with you the covenant loyalty that he swore to your ancestors; he will love you, bless you, and multiply you."

The Bible tells us it takes faith coupled with hard work to succeed and also imparts many valuable lessons I have found applicable to working with employees, vendors, and customers in ways that assure prosperity. For instance, Jesus expounded that we are here to serve others. His teachings that we are put on this earth to love and serve others are not idle words. They are not meant to be spoken in church on Sunday but not practiced in the workplace. There is no imaginary line that separates my behavior in business from my private life. Personally, I don't adhere to the belief that "business is different," and that therefore a different code of ethics can be applied.

On a lighter note, I'm reminded about the story of a man who arrived at the Gates of Heaven. An angel asked him to state his occupation. "I've been a minister for forty-five years," he answered. The angel welcomed him into heaven and led him to a modest house where he would be quartered for eternity.

A second man approached the Gates of Heaven, stating he had driven a taxi in New York City for the past forty-two years. An accompanying angel took him to a stately mansion to be his home for eternity.

The minister was upset to see the taxi driver receive such a fine home while he did not. "I was a minister and served the Lord for forty-five years," he exclaims to the angel. "And he was a taxicab driver. There must be a mistake!"

"No," replies the angel. "Around here, we go by results. When you gave your sermons, people slept. When he drove a taxi, people prayed."

I also go by results, and I can attest that when you do business by the Good Book, you get results. It works like this: Adhering to the principle of loving and caring for others, my company focuses on providing the best value and service we possibly can. Companies that do this are generally successful. Likewise, we're interested in attracting and retaining the *right* people. Once they come aboard, our objective is to provide them with opportunities to succeed. This is what gives me the most satisfaction. Nothing is more rewarding to me than knowing that our people are prospering and able to provide their families with such things as fine educations and new homes–all of which result from the leap of faith we took when we began this company.

My company is also my ministry. It provides not only an opportunity for me to conform to the lessons from the Bible, but also a platform on which to serve God by being his ambassador in the business world. As 2 Corinthians 5:20 says, "So we are ambassadors for Christ, since God is making his appeal through us; we entreat you on behalf of Christ, be reconciled to God."

Our pastor at Union Memorial United Methodist Church, Dr. Lynn Mims, has visited our company on several occasions and knows this successful enterprise is built on biblical teachings. In 1999, Dr. Mims called me at my office and asked if we could get Thelma at home to join us in a conference call. When she joined us, Dr. Mims talked about a vision God had given him. He said: "I want you to take the principles you practice at your company, and use them to conduct a Sunday school class for businesspeople. When you do, others who follow your lead can also prosper by doing good."

Having been active church members for more than twenty years, we wanted to support Dr. Mims and our church. But due to our busy schedules, we were concerned about making such a time-consuming, long-term commitment. Our skepticism was merited–we were already finding it difficult to get to church on time, never mind committing to being there promptly and prepared to diligently teach a class every Sunday. "We'll have to pray on it," we told him.

That night, Thelma reminded me of what Jesus said in Luke 12:48: "From everyone to whom much has been given, much will be required; and from the one to whom much has been entrusted, even more will be demanded." We prayed and God showed us that this was what he wanted us to do. In the morning, we called Dr. Mims to tell him we were ready to start the Sunday school class immediately.

Today, our class, Doing Business by the Book, has been well received and attendance keeps climbing. Forty-plus people come each Sunday, including a wide range of businesspeople–some just starting new companies, others successful business leaders. Past and current governors of Missouri have attended; other dignitaries have included U.S. senators, U.S. congressmen, members of city and county councils, and clergymen from other denominations. We encourage class participation, and attendees frequently give testimonies. In this open forum, attendees receive counsel on how to apply business lessons from the Bible and, in turn, prosper. Most important, they understand the importance of learning the Word of God and their responsibility to be an ambassador of God. Thelma and I have totally submitted ourselves to God, and class members know that if they follow God's Word, he will energize them too and they will prosper.

Our classes have been so well received, we want to impart these lessons to everyone. I am reminded of what Thelma recently advised a young woman: "Give your full tithe to God because it's not really yours. All of it belongs to him anyway." She then added, "Besides, he's only asking for 10 percent of it."

My wife and I feel we've been blessed so we can become a blessing. The lessons we continue to learn from the Bible make us prosper, and it's our responsibility to share that blessing with others. It isn't something we keep for ourselves. It didn't belong to us. It was given to us. For this reason, we share it freely with others.

Our popular Doing Business by the Book class is the catalyst for writing this book. I want to share what we have learned so you too may be blessed. And when you are, it will be your turn to share your blessings with others.

1

THE ENTREPRENEURIAL SPIRIT

Give, and it will be given to you. A good measure, pressed down, shaken together, running over, will be put into your lap; for the measure you give will be the measure you get back.

—Luke 6:38

In the dictionary, an entrepreneur is defined as "one who organizes, manages, and assumes the risk of a business." While the definition is valid, it seems sterile without a reference to the entrepreneurial spirit.

When I think about the big leap I took by venturing out on my own, I had more on my mind than just organizing, managing, and assuming the risk of a business. My thoughts focused on Noah's faith in God when he built the ark. Genesis 6:13–16 describes God telling Noah that he would destroy all flesh because the earth was filled with violence. Then God instructed Noah to build an ark measuring 300 cubits in length, or about 450 feet. The ark's width should be 75 feet and it should stand 45 feet high.

Imagine how much Noah had to trust God to take on such a task. Working with crude tools, Noah, a farmer from Ur, and his sons, Shem, Ham, and Japheth, constructed this huge vessel–the biggest ever built in its day. Noah built it exactly to God's specifications, never deviating from his instructions. The ark was supposed to save Noah and his family from an impending flood, yet there were no clouds in the sky that showed any sign of even a rain shower. Still, Noah and his sons worked day and night on the ark. People came from near and far to see the four driven men build the huge ark in the desert. Neighbors and visitors ridiculed and cursed Noah, yet he never abandoned his faith in God.

True, starting my own company was a miniscule task compared to Noah's. I was the son of a mechanic, who was also a man of the soil. My father worked a small farm–consisting of a couple of cows, a few chickens, and some hogs–to feed his family of ten. Even though I had received my business degree from Central Missouri State University in 1973 and had held various sales and marketing positions with Union Pacific Railroad and Federal Express, people didn't hesitate to question me: "What do you know about owning your own business? How could you quit a good job to start your own company?"

When you dare to have ambitions, people tend to ridicule you; they become vocal about why you cannot and even should not attempt to pursue your dream. Some well-meaning friends and family members are trying to protect you, while others may be jealous that you might succeed. Few have the same belief in you that you have in yourself. There will always be someone who wants to rain on your parade, but an entrepreneur can't be swayed by other people's standards. Don't let them put you into a box. If you buy into what's expected of you, you'll be restricted by others' limitations. Better you should be guided by God's unlimited promise. We've all been told: "Finish your education, get a good job, work for a good company, and you'll have a great life." In other words, work all your life, get a gold watch, and retire.

This message is repeated and reinforced by people who are all too willing to tell us what they think we should do. Friends, teachers, and even college professors continually reinforce it, and then parents confirm this message to their children by being living examples of it. It takes a leap of faith to raise yourself above what others expect of you. The hardest thing to do is take that first step to overcome your fears and self-doubt, especially when you're surrounded by doubting Thomases who constantly reinforce those fears, based on their personal beliefs.

Becoming a player in the world of Information Technology (IT), which was a new revolution in the 1980s, presented challenges to all who sought entry, and, in particular, an African-American. To this day, I can visualize the frowns on the faces of friends and family who said, "You know they won't let you do that." I wondered, "Who are *they*?"

Following about ten years of employment in corporate America, in 1984 I started my own company, Transportation Business Specialists. My transition to the role of sole proprietor was difficult; it meant no longer having a supervisor to rely on, no steady paycheck, and no expense account. The umbilical cord was cut; I relinquished the safety net of a large corporation. Along with a second entity, a sister company I created called Transport Administrative Services, we provided services to the transportation industry by locating inefficiencies in the commercial freight industry. These auditing services revealed how much the railroads were losing for undercharges as opposed to overcharges. At the time, many companies provided overcharge services informing customers that ship by rail when they were charged too much, but nobody had ever taken our approach and worked the other end of the equation. Consequently, we were engaged to do an undercharge audit of three years' worth of freight bills for Union Pacific Railroad, which meant that my company would manage $15 billion of rate information for a single client.

The only way to handle that amount of information was through a local area network to link all of their operations, so we built what was at the time the biggest network in St. Louis. After I learned the benefits of effectively integrating technology to solve business problems, I formed my current company, World Wide Technology, in 1990 with an investment of $250,000, hard-earned money from my two earlier ventures.

WWT wasn't exactly an "overnight success." We had our peaks and valleys, and although I never missed a single payroll, many weeks I didn't receive my own paycheck. Employees always came first. At one point in 1993, things were so tight, a collection company repossessed my car right from our parking lot. Fortunately, I ran after the car and was able to stop it so I could retrieve my briefcase from the trunk.

When friends and acquaintances asked my wife, Thelma, about our new venture, and she explained what our IT company did, they'd roll their eyes. Once a woman told Thelma, "Well, you guys must like living on the edge." We quickly learned to throw conventional wisdom out the window, knowing that what the world thinks is wise, God thinks is foolish.

It is always darkest before the dawn, and even in the most discouraging times, I never lost my faith in God. I was in his hands, and I always knew the Lord would look after me. I constantly reminded myself that when God told Abraham to take his only son to the altar to sacrifice him, Abraham did as he was told. Imagine the confusion in Abraham's mind–a man who was incredibly old when his son was born, and yet he was prepared to sacrifice him. At the time, Abraham didn't know God would have him sacrifice a lamb instead. If Abraham could have such faith in God, I believed I too could trust God to look after me.

Throughout my life, I have followed examples set by individuals in the Bible, such men as Abraham, Noah, and David, who had been given a charge to do God's work. And I, through my business and my daily life, have a charge to do God's work, to be obedient and find favor with the Lord.

As the Bible tells us, we are here to sow seed into people's lives. In Luke 6:38, Christ says: "Give, and it will be given to you. A good measure, pressed down, shaken together, running over, will be put into your lap; for the measure you give will be the measure you get back." I live my life by these words. My objective in business is not driven by how much money I may make. I seek to serve and to give to others.

In business, my biggest job as CEO and owner of my company is to serve others. My charge is to serve the employees of this organization and serve them well. In my company, I strive to nurture service and commitment to others, an attitude that places others before us. We abide by this philosophy rather than participating in a self-serving culture, and it permeates externally to customers and suppliers. Then, like a pebble cast into a lake, its ripples eventually reach the shore. Trust and loyalty communicated to others assures long-term success.

Jesus devoted his life to serving others. Even at the Last Supper, Jesus demonstrated that he was here to serve when he knelt to wash the feet of his disciples. In doing so, Jesus humbled himself, because Hebrew culture viewed the washing of feet as the lowliest of acts. Some of his disciples were so embarrassed, they argued and refused to have their Lord and Savior serve them. But Jesus was there to serve, just as he was there to sacrifice his life for us.

Similarly, the success of a business owner is dependent upon his or her desire to serve others. I believe this philosophy of servitude epitomizes the entrepreneurial spirit.

2

INTEGRITY

A good name is to be chosen rather than great riches, and favor is better than silver or gold.

—Proverbs 22:1

In biblical days, most people did not read or write, so business was conducted based on the spoken word. And just as a written document is binding today in a court of law, so was an oral agreement in the early days. (An oral agreement is also binding under current law; however, in the absence of a willing witness, it is difficult to prove.) The way I see it, a businessperson is obligated to be honor-bound to live by the spoken word. To paraphrase an old cliché, a man is only as good as his word. Standing behind your word is every bit as relevant today as it was when a handshake was all that it took to seal a business deal.

We are told in 2 Corinthians 5:17–20 that we are ambassadors for God. As ambassadors of God, we represent him, each and every day of our lives. In this capacity, each of us has a twenty-four-hour-a-day commitment, on and off the job. Yet, not all businesspeople recognize their ambassadorship. To gain an edge over a competitor, many people are prone to give in to the temptation to engage in unprincipled practices.

"It's business," they claim. "It's a cutthroat, dog-eat-dog world. To get ahead, I have to get the other guy before he gets me!"

They rationalize, "You don't understand. It's okay because this is business."

No matter how fierce the competition, this attitude has no place in the workplace. Personal values should never be put aside—nor should standards be lowered to the level of the unscrupulous. As a business owner, I have an obligation to lead by example. This position puts me in the limelight: My actions are observed, and people know when I do right by them.

My wife is my partner in life, and she and I believe my company represents who we are. Together, we have prayed and have dedicated our business to God. It is our ministry, and through it, we are doing God's work. It is our temple, and by serving our employees, they, in turn, serve our customers and suppliers. Only with integrity can we successfully serve so many others.

During the early years of my company, we endured many setbacks. When we were hard-pressed for money, we could have cut corners in subtle ways, to turn a profit. We all know of business owners who manipulate their books, cut back slightly on the quality of their product or services, and find excuses to avoid properly compensating deserving employees. The temptation to profit at someone else's expense is widespread.

For instance, a short while ago, a customer submitted an overpayment of about $1 million to our company. We could have easily buried this error in our books and kept quiet about it. But it was not the right thing to do. Just as we taught our children to pay for an item at a store's checkout counter, even if the salesclerk has overlooked it, we apply the same principle in business. Consequently, we sent a check for the full amount of the overpayment to our customer with a letter of explanation.

In business, there are always temptations to do the wrong thing. The Bible addresses temptations (Luke 4:1–11), describing how Jesus spent forty days in the wilderness during which time the devil tried again and again to tempt him. During this period, Jesus ate nothing and was famished. The devil said to him, "If you are the Son of God, command this stone to become a loaf of bread." Jesus answered, "One does not live by bread alone."

Then Jesus was offered the wealth of all the kingdoms of the world, but in exchange, he must worship the devil. Jesus replied that he would worship and serve only God.

Next, the devil challenged Jesus to leap from the pinnacle of the temple, suggesting that if he were the Son of God, the angels would protect him from injury.

Jesus answered him, "It is said, 'Do not put the Lord your God to the test.' "

Following Jesus' example when he refused to submit to temptation, I don't believe in compromising values, regardless of how convenient it may seem at the time. It doesn't matter how many other people do wrong things, each of us must still do what's right. We must do what we say and live by our word.

A person's reputation is a most valued asset, one to be treasured. One's reputation is based on whether one keeps his or her word. We are taught in Proverbs 22:1: "A good name is to be chosen rather than great riches, and favor is better than silver or gold." It takes a lifetime to build a good reputation, but it can be lost overnight.

And what better heritage can parents pass on to their children than a good name? I believe this applies to a company as well. Senior managers must conduct themselves with integrity, because ultimately that integrity passes on to the next generation of managers. As my company's CEO, I do not take this responsibility lightly.

While it is true that I prosper from the success of my company, my goal is to build a business to benefit current and future employees–men and women who will work at this company when I am no longer here. In years to come, the prosperity of those people will rest, in part, on the foundation of integrity we build today.

3

DELEGATION

The kingdom of heaven is like a mustard seed that someone took and sowed in his field. It is the smallest of all seeds, but when it has grown it is the greatest of shrubs and becomes a tree.

—Matthew 13:31

There are many examples of delegation throughout the Scriptures. For, instance while leading his people in the wilderness, a major portion of Moses' day was spent settling disputes among his followers. Observing this, his father-in-law, Jethro, advised him to delegate. In Exodus 18:17–27, Jethro told Moses to stop wearing himself out by attempting to do everything himself. He suggested that Moses surround himself with able, trustworthy men and appoint them to manage others. These trusted individuals would serve as judges on trivial matters and only important matters would be presented to Moses. "You are placing too much burden upon yourself by attempting to do everything," Jethro warned.

In the way that Moses had initially failed to delegate, many sole proprietors also overburden themselves. And they too wear themselves out with a heavy task. Conversely, successful owners of companies employing many people take advantage of leverage, which permits them to accomplish considerably more. They do this by delegating responsibilities. Jesus also recognized that he could accomplish more by delegating to others. In Matthew 10, Jesus authorized his twelve disciples to cast out unclean spirits and to cure disease and sickness. They were instructed to neither solicit Gentiles nor enter any town of the Samaritans, but instead go to the lost sheep in the house of Israel. Jesus asked them to proclaim the good news: "The kingdom of heaven has come near." Their mission was to cure the sick, raise the dead, cleanse the lepers, and to cast out demons. Jesus did not pay his disciples and said they should not accept any payments for their work. And when they entered a town or village, they should find out who in it was worthy and who was not.

Jesus' disciples were ordinary men from diverse occupations—a fisherman might sit at his feet beside a tax collector. Most importantly, they were good men whom he trusted and gave enormous responsibility. Through the scripture I have learned to delegate responsibility to individuals based on their attitude, work ethic, and principles. I believe it comes down to trusting the right people—those who have integrity, loyalty, and commitment. I look for these qualities before I place people in leadership roles. While there may be other candidates with better résumés, I listen carefully to what a person receives in his heart. Through conversation, what he is receiving in the Gospel comes out. Luke 6:45 says that a good person speaks from the heart, and if we listen carefully, we will pick up on this. With this in mind, what a person is internalizing means more to me than their credentials.

Several times, we hired people who looked good on paper but didn't work out. On the other hand, we've put good, solid businesspeople into positions even when they didn't have all the necessary technical skills. We believed they had good core business principles and understood how to work with people. Once on the job, nearly everyone learns the necessary technological skills.

In Matthew 13:31, a parable of Jesus is quoted: "The kingdom of heaven is like a mustard seed that someone took and sowed in his field. It is the smallest of all seeds, but when it has grown it is the greatest of shrubs and becomes a tree." A businessperson delegates assignments to people, and like the planting of a small mustard seed that becomes a tree and branches out, the work blossoms and multiplies. Great organizations blossom through the efforts of many.

In the beginning, the owner of a small start-up company may have no one to delegate to. Consequently, the owner does everything–from secretarial chores to selling and servicing customers. Later, when he employs workers, he has become so accustomed to doing everything himself that he finds it hard to delegate. He thinks, "If I want it done right, I need to do it myself." As a result, they end up delegating only menial assignments, keeping meaningful responsibilities for themselves.

I understand it's not easy for an entrepreneur to let go: He has already developed his own personal way of doing things. Frequently this is because a company owner lets his ego get in his way and believes nobody can match his expertise–especially in a business he built from scratch. I have a special word for this attitude that I call "edgo." It means edging God out. I say, "Better to let go and let God." To grow a business, you can't let false pride govern you. As Proverbs 16:18 says, "Pride goes before destruction, and a haughty spirit before a fall."

At some point, you have to let go and trust your people. You sow the seed of trust by giving trust. I truly believe delegation begins with trusting others–followed by letting go. In a sizeable company, a good leader must trust key individuals to assume responsibility for various segments of the business. Only in this way can strong partnership relationships be built. Through this trust and confidence a company can grow exponentially. Once the owner relaxes his or her tight grip on operations, that small mustard seed grows and branches out.

As CEO, I must surround myself with specialists from different areas who have expertise that exceeds mine, and I must rely on their advice. This requires me to have explicit trust in these individuals, because I must rely on them to operate their own organizations within the company. With everyone aboard sharing a vision, our mutual plan serves as our roadmap into the future. Our company has a matrix that allows us to use an effective reporting system to measure and monitor each organization's success for profitability. At weekly finance meetings, we review every department of the company. This way, everyone can pull together and receive support from others. Although I bring wise counsel together to determine what is in the best interest of the organization, as CEO, I am responsible for the final decision.

4

STRIVING FOR EXCELLENCE

When I look at your heavens, the work of your fingers, the moon and the stars that you have established; What are human beings that you are mindful of them, mortals that you care for them? Yet you have made them a little lower than God, and crowned them with glory and honor.

—Psalms 8:3–5

The verse quoted above says that we are created in God's image and reminds us that we should strive for excellence in doing his work. Although only the Lord is capable of perfection, we should endeavor to do our best. When I launched my business, I pledged that it would excel in serving people, both in and outside of the company. I was determined to provide the best service possible to our employees, as well as to our vendors and customers. Perfection may be impossible, but our objective reminds us to continually strive for improvement.

A commitment to excellence starts at the top of an organization. A CEO must demonstrate he or she is dedicated to making it happen. Initially, the CEO does this by communicating to employees that anything less than excellence is unacceptable. Next, the CEO's actions set the pace, and as we are told in 1 Peter 5:3, we should lead by example.

To attain such lofty standards, we have to bring in the right talent. They must be trained and nurtured to excel. In time, every person in the organization shares the CEO's philosophy of excellence. When those who aren't committed leave the company, others come in to replace them. A commitment to excellence may start in the highest office of an organization, but it must trickle down the corporate ladder to every employee. The demand for excellence permeates through the organization to customers. The bottom line is that each and every one of us in the company works for the customer. The customer is our employer. At my company, we believe this concept so much, every paycheck bears this imprint: "A satisfied customer made this check possible." And those are not idle words, believe you me.

Striving for excellence isn't something you do for a while, then stop, then continue some other time at your convenience. It's a long-term proposition. In fact, in the short run, excellence can be very inconvenient: It takes a costly investment that doesn't immediately result in profit. Often, this means a decision must be made to live with short-term losses while waiting for long-term gains.

In the case of a publicly owned company, the investment community can apply tremendous pressure to produce quarterly profits. This outside persuasion sometimes tempts management to think short-term, reduce expenditures, and forgo quality. Management may be reluctant to report disappointing quarterly statements to shareholders. But the demand put on management for three-month gains isn't necessarily good for a company's long-term interests. It should be noted that some shareholders are driven to pursue short-term profits in order to hike up the price of the stock. Frequently their sole interest is to realize a quick profit and invest elsewhere. But the company's senior managers want what's best for the company in the long run–because their careers depend on their employer's future solvency. This course also serves the best interests of long-term investors.

Investment bankers have approached our company to "take us public," always with promises of making us very rich. Each time so far, I've turned them down. Why? I believe the stock market lives for the present, while I live for the unseen: I foresee a future of unfathomable opportunity–for my family, employees, vendors, customers, and even for our technology. Outside investors generally don't tolerate this risk of capital. Still, someday down the road, a public offering might make sense–the future may introduce other factors to consider.

It takes conviction to resist the demands of short-term thinkers. Indeed, guiding a business takes patience, because great businesses are not built overnight. Nor is excellence achieved in one fell swoop. Attaining excellence is not a strategy; it's a process–a never-ending process that demands continual improvement.

After Moses died, God spoke to Joshua and directed him to lead the Israelites across the Jordan River. God clearly instructs Joshua to carry out his mission, and do exactly as told–by the book! Joshua must stay on course; he must never veer even slightly right or left. By staying focused on God's orders, Joshua was assured of prosperity and success. Likewise, as creatures in the image of God, we should work assiduously, always striving to achieve excellence.

Imagine an entire organization, from the person at the top, down through the ranks to the most recently hired recruit in an entry-level position–every man and woman focused on excellence. Think about all such an organization could achieve and contribute to the world. As God promised Joshua, this formula will generate prosperity and success.

5

ADAPTING TO CHANGE

For in hope we are saved. Now hope that is seen is not hope. For who hopes for what is seen? But if we hope for what we do not see, we wait for it with patience.

—Romans 8:24–25

Adapting to change is a recurring biblical theme; the subject first appears in God's creation of the heavens and the earth. God created a universe that is constantly changing. The galaxies, stars, and planets are in a state of perpetual motion–vast bodies that never remain still. Our planet revolves around the sun–day is followed by night, and seasons come and go. Likewise, a peek into the microscopic world of tiny drops of pond water reveals diminutive worlds, each consisting of countless numbers of microorganisms busily moving to and fro.

Life itself is about change. From conception to birth through many years of life to death, our bodies and minds continually change. Similarly, each day differs from the previous day. Change is a natural condition encompassing every facet of our lives.

I view change as one of the wonders of life. If every day were a duplicate of the preceding day, life would indeed be monotonous. But change is what makes life interesting–it's always something new. Change is what keeps the media in business. Without it, there would be nothing to report on the nightly news and in the daily newspapers.

Although we live in an ever-changing universe, many people have a tendency to resist change. Why? Because we must venture into the unknown, which requires risk-taking. It takes faith to venture into the unknown; the Bible abounds with examples of such faith. Hebrews 11:7–18 describes the faith of Noah, and Abraham, first with Noah, who had respected God's warning of an unseen flood and with his sons built an ark. Then Abraham's faith is revealed when he obeyed God and set out for a place where he was to receive his inheritance, not knowing where he was going. Abraham lived in tents in a foreign land, and later so did his sons, Isaac and Jacob. All the while, Abraham looked forward to his promise of a city with foundations whose architect and builder was God. For his faith, God gave the power of procreation to Abraham, although he was too old and his wife, Sarah, was barren. Consequently, Abraham had many, many descendants, which the Scriptures describe as being "as many as the stars of heaven and as the innumerable grains of sand by the seashore."

Chapter 11 in the Book of Hebrews also enumerates other biblical events that required faith, including the Israelites' passing through the Red Sea as they were being pursued by the Egyptians. It also took tremendous faith to believe that the walls of Jericho would fall after they had been encircled for seven days.

We are taught to believe in what we see rather than what we don't see. Obviously, more faith is required to believe in what we *don't* see. Faith is the substance of things hoped for, the evidence of things not seen. This is explained in Romans 8:24–25: "For hope we were saved. Now hope that is seen is not hope. For who hopes for what is seen? But if we hope for what we do not see, we wait for it with patience." Faith and hope require patience because great change does not come overnight. Of course, as we are reminded in James 2:17, faith and hard work get the best results. Prayer alone will not suffice. You must reinforce your belief with hard work.

Years ago when I worked for Federal Express as senior account executive, I was tapped as Salesman of the Year and made a member of the company's hall of fame. At the podium, founder and CEO Fred Smith presented me with a trophy–an ice bucket that featured my engraved initials. When I looked inside the bucket, I saw nothing, and to me, that was a defining moment. I asked myself, Is this what I wanted out of life? A pat on the back, and an "Atta boy, get back out there and get 'em again."

My sales quota was raised from 100 to 150 percent, putting the carrot out there a little farther. I thought, I don't want to wake up when I'm seventy or eighty and wonder why I didn't do more.

At the time, my wife and I had two small children, a mortgage, and a small bank account. We were living paycheck to paycheck with all the trappings of success that keep you locked into a job.

I knew a man from Kansas City who owned a consulting firm and was getting ready to retire. His firm did auditing and reviewing of freight bill charges, and from my previous experience with Union Pacific, I felt comfortable making him an offer for his business–with nothing down. My offer was accepted. So I left my $65,000-a-year job with its car allowance, expense account, and excellent package of fringe benefits. I was on my own–removed from the security blanket that comes with being a Fortune 500 company employee. Needless to say, it was a dramatic change.

My hope for a bright future and my courage to venture out on my own hinged on my faith in God. I firmly believed what I read in the Scriptures. I remembered passages like 2 Timothy 1:7 telling us that "God did not give us a spirit of cowardice, but rather a spirit of power and of love and of self-discipline." These words removed any fears or self-doubt I might have possessed. It was clear in my mind that my belief in God, coupled with the desire to work hard to serve others, meant I was destined to succeed.

I found the Twenty-third Psalm to be particularly inspiring, and I frequently read it to lift my spirits. My company had its share of hard times and, like other small start-up companies, there were enormous hurdles to overcome. During these periods, I turned to these words to affirm my belief that God is always with me. To this day, this psalm provides me with comfort, assuring me I cannot fail.

In 1984 I left corporate America to start my first business venture, Transport Administrative Services, which located inefficiencies in the commercial freight industry. The company audited railroad invoices; however, through a series of changes that involved switching totally to technology, my company has gone from the highway to the superhighway. World Wide Technology was started in 1990, and today, our core business is providing solutions to companies in many industries through technology. Making the switch was an enormous undertaking. Because we made this change, our client base is no longer limited to serving only the railroad industry. That same year, a woman from the Small Business Administration's St. Louis office approached us to see whether, as a small minority-owned company, we would be interested in applying our technology services to the federal government. Since that initial meeting, we have developed several government customers, including the Department of Defense, Department of Transportation, and the Department of Agriculture. Due to the rapid growth that we enjoyed early on, we became too big to qualify as a minority-owned small business under the jurisdiction of the SBA. But we'll be forever grateful to the SBA for opening doors that enabled us to develop key relationships. I give high marks to the SBA. Today, our list of clients includes Southwestern Bell, Bell Atlantic, GTE, Cingular, Verizon, and Lucent.

Adapting to change is a fundamental factor in determining the success of major companies. For instance, DuPont was the world's largest manufacturer of gunpowder and America's largest supplier from the War of 1812 through World War I. During the Civil War, DuPont supplied gunpowder to both the North and the South. Back in the 1840s, a company known as the Pony Express became today's American Express. It wasn't until 1891 that the first American Express Travelers Cheque was issued. And the first American Express card was issued in 1958. When the company known today as IBM was founded in 1914, it was called the Computing-Tabulating-Recording Company, a manufacturer of butcher scales. It wasn't until 1924 that it was renamed International Business Machines. In 1948, Honda got its start as a motorcycle manufacturer, but today the company is better known for its automobiles. A long list of great companies have thrived over the years because they recognized that change represents opportunity. I guess they must have agreed with renowned advertising executive (BBDO) Bruce Barton (1886–1967), who said, "Keep changing. When you're through changing, you're through."

These days World Wide Technology is deeply entrenched in

the Internet industry, the fastest-changing industry ever. Consider this: The Internet is growing faster than all other technologies that preceded it. Thirty-eight years after radio came out, it had 50 million listeners. Television took only thirteen years to acquire the same size audience. The Internet hit the 50 million–user mark in a mere four years! In 1994, only 3 million people were Internet-connected. By 1999, 67.5 million U.S. computers were online—a total of 92 million users—up 50 percent from the previous year. At the time I write this, there are more than 180 million users in the United States and Canada. You can be sure bigger numbers will dwarf this number in the not-too-distant future.

Certainly I could have chosen a career doing something else that didn't involve so much change. I could have also stayed in the railroad auditing field, or for that matter, remained at Federal Express, where I was on track to move up the corporate ladder and have a successful career in management. But instead I made certain risk-taking decisions and ventured out on my own. Only with my deep faith in God could I face such change head-on. I was armed with the belief that he was always with me.

6

FINDING A NICHE

No one can serve two masters.

—Matthew 6:24

It takes vast resources to dominate even a portion of a marketplace. Even a huge multibillion dollar company can't offer something for everyone. Instead, companies look for ways to fill a niche–a route even small start-ups can take. Good news for the entrepreneur: Many niches are too small for giant corporations to consider. For example, a mass marketer such as General Motors isn't likely to go after the Rolls Royce customer because the market is limited to a relatively small number of very wealthy potential purchasers.

Finding a niche is a smart way to start a business, and that's what I did when I left corporate America. When I did my homework, I observed many companies auditing freight invoices to identify overcharges by railroads, but nobody was auditing on the other side of the coin–looking for underpayments due the railroads. Hence, not only did I fill a niche, I developed a way to provide a service with efficiencies that future competitors could not easily duplicate. To keep ahead of the competition, we committed ourselves to make continual improvements so we could maintain a lead over anyone trying to copy us. As Andrew Carnegie said, "The first man gets the oyster, the second man gets the shell."

My company focused on a particular industry—railroads—and because I'd been employed by Union Pacific for several years, I was familiar with the business. It's important to realize I wasn't trying to attract airline, trucking, or any other transportation companies. Nor did I approach companies in other industries that might have had similar problems. I understood the meaning of Matthew 6:24: "No one can serve two masters." With this in mind, I audited only payments that were due but not being collected by the railroads. In the early stages of my business, it was very clear that my company had one master to serve—nothing else was going to distract us from our mission. Why did we make no attempt to try our hand at auditing underpayments for anyone else? Because, as specialists, we could deliver outstanding service to railroads.

Finding a niche was just the beginning. With Union Pacific as our one and only account, we worked day and night to make sure we took very good care of our sole customer. We knew if we lost it, we'd be out of business. I also knew it would take a lot of hard work to make a success of our fledlging enterprise—plus a strong faith in God. Never forget, it takes both. Hard work alone won't do it, and neither will faith alone. This is distinctly stated in James 2:14–17: "What good is it, my brothers and sisters, if you say you have faith but do not have works? Can faith save you? If a brother or sister is naked and lacks daily food, and one of you says to them, 'Go in peace; keep warm and eat your fill,' and yet you do not supply their bodily needs, what is the good of that? So faith by itself, if it has no works, is dead."

My previous employer, Federal Express, is a major Fortune 500 company today, and it too got its start by finding a niche in the marketplace. Look what the company provides: an overnight mail delivery that's faster than the U.S. Post Office daily mail. Most U.S. mail arrives within forty-eight hours and costs only a postage stamp, but for $15 a letter, Federal Express delivers overnight! Evidently, many people are willing to pay a very high premium to be assured that their mail arrives the following day–proof that Federal Express found a void to fill in the marketplace.

Many of today's largest and most successful companies started as niche players. Wal-Mart, the world's largest retailer, discovered its niche back in its early days when it opened stores in small towns across America. From the 1950s through the 1970s, the company's strategy was to cater to the needs of people in small towns who didn't have the opportunity to shop at department stores and discount chains located in large metropolitan areas. Only years later did Wal-Mart decide to expand into larger communities.

In the late 1960s, just when everyone thought AT&T had the monopoly on telephone service, along came niche player MCI with a strategy to provide an alternative long-distance telephone service. Likewise, Microsoft got its start by having a singular focus on making software for PCs. (At the time, IBM hadn't given much thought to the software or PC business.)

In the back of every neophyte entrepreneur's mind lurks worry: How can a small niche player survive against giant, well-established companies with deep pockets and enormous resources? Needless to say, the big boys didn't get where they are by being shrinking violets. In my early days, I rid myself of worrisome thoughts by rereading the story of David. This inspirational narrative in 1 Samuel 17 tells of the Philistines, Israel's archenemy, and their secret weapon, Goliath, who thoroughly intimidated the Israelite army. No Israelite soldier dared step forward to fight Goliath–and for good reason. At a height of six cubits and a span, Goliath was literally a giant, standing nine feet, nine inches tall. His 5,000-shekel coat of bronze weighed 125 pounds! The Philistines stood on one side of a mountain with a valley separating them from the Israelites. Goliath, in full armor, challenged the troops of Israel: "Choose a man for yourselves, and let him come down to me. If he is able to fight with me and kill me, then we will be your servants; but if I prevail against him and kill him, then you shall be our servants and serve us."

Only David, a shepherd boy, volunteered to fight the gigantic Philistine. King Saul had tried to help by equipping David with a bronze helmet and armor, but David was unable to walk in them. Hence, David faced Goliath with only his sling and a shepherd's bag that contained five stones. Defying overwhelmingly great odds, so singularly focused was David that he used but a single stone to slay his horrendous adversary. This same intensity of focus is required for the small niche player to hold his own against today's industry giants.

Some entrepreneurs find a niche and build their entire careers around it. To others, that niche is merely a stepping stone leading to other business ventures. In my case, we started with one large customer, Union Pacific, and later audited underpayments for three other railroads. That meant four out of seven of the nation's largest railroads were our customers. Only later did my company branch out to seek other niches in the field of technology. Although my company's revenues grew from zero to over $1 billion in twelve years, we applied patience, we crawled before we walked, and only later were we able to break into a run.

7

GOOD LEADERSHIP IS SERVING OTHERS

. . . whoever wishes to become great among you must be your servant, and whoever wishes to be first among you must be slave of all. For the Son of Man came not to be served but to serve, and to give his life a ransom for many.

—Mark 10:43–45

Jesus gives these instructions to his twelve disciples, and I base my management philosophy on these words. Because his mission was to serve, so is mine. My serving starts with the five-hundred-plus people associated with my company.

This means I must dedicate myself to place the needs of our employees above my own. I am here to help them succeed. Consequently, a high percentage of my time and energy is spent coaching, advising, and supporting our people. This effort is backed up by large amounts of money invested in training and developing people to further their careers. I make myself available to them during the workday so they can tap into my business experience. Plus I provide them with access to my vast reservoir of business contacts. What's all this for? So they can grow and realize their full potential.

We've all been around bosses who think their rank entitles them to be served by their subordinates. A manager consumed with self-importance may think his title alone should automatically assure respect. "Serve others?" he asks. "I'm the boss. They serve me." He just doesn't get it.

Not only is this attitude counterproductive, it hurts morale and builds a barrier between management and the workforce. It creates an us versus them antagonism. This robs the staff of their incentive to do their best. Employees who feel their boss doesn't care about them respond by not caring about the boss, or for that matter, the organization itself. Consequently, they couldn't care less whether their boss succeeds. So what do they do? They exert only enough effort to remain on the payroll–their work is simply a job and pride of ownership flies out the window. That self-absorbed manager will never enjoy more than mediocre performance from his staff.

While many business executives hold titles that indicate leadership, few truly know how to lead. Getting people to follow orders is not leading! A true leader inspires people to do their best. A leader's people want to be successful because they sincerely care about their company and its leaders. They care because they know management cares about them. They work hard because they don't want to let their leader down.

It's common for people in leadership positions to think *they* are the ones who should be served. This has long been the conventional thinking in business. But the truly effective leader knows the reverse is true. Good leaders understand their role is to serve their people. Serving others is not only the best way to the top, it's the only effective way to stay there. Once you've been promoted up the corporate ladder your avenues to serve others are multiplied.

Over the years, I've worked around several major Fortune 500 companies, and based on my experience with others, figured out what kind of leader I'd like to be. The leaders I liked least placed serving their own agenda before the needs of others. This was evident in their every action. It showed in the high salaries, generous bonuses, and stock options they made sure they received–even when red ink was flowing. Astonishingly, they rewarded themselves with performance bonuses no matter how poorly they performed.

These same individuals established barriers that distanced them from their people. They put themselves into lush offices on executive floors, in ivory towers with layers of management below to separate themselves from rank and file employees. Exorbitant perks–private jets, unlimited expense accounts, private parking spaces, executive dining rooms, executive bathrooms–made these managers the elite few, the privileged. By comparison, all others were the working class–second-class citizens, peons. The condescending demeanor of such a boss is conspicuous, offensive, and demoralizing.

I vowed I would not emulate that example, and today our company strives to eliminate barriers that separate and divide people. In our early years when times were lean, I made sure every employee received his or her full paycheck–even when it meant forgoing my own. To this day, there are no executive dining rooms, private bathrooms, or personal parking spaces. Who parks in the best space? Whoever arrives first at work, that's who.

Sadly, some people start at the bottom, work their way to the top, and then believe they've earned the right to sit back and savor the rich bounties they believe come with the job. "I've paid the price," they say. "Bring on the perks. It's my turn now to get what's due me!"

I have no problem with top officers who are handsomely compensated in accordance with their contributions to the company. Generous compensation packages are needed to attract and keep top talent. What I don't like are senior managers who expect to be placed on a pedestal while obedient subordinates scramble to serve them. In my experience, the ones who do their jobs best are those who understand that good leadership and serving others are synonymous.

I object to the myth these so-called leaders perpetuate: that those down the chain of command must serve those at the top.

John 13 tells the story of Jesus washing the feet of his disciples at the Last Supper, knowing that his hour had come to depart from this world and go to the Father. By washing their feet, Jesus was making a statement that we are here to serve others. If the greatest leader of all time could humbly serve his disciples in this manner, shouldn't we follow his example? I take this lesson to heart, and I go to my office every day knowing I am there to serve others.

In Matthew 22:36–40, Jesus is asked, " 'Teacher, which commandment in the law is the greatest?' He said to him, 'You shall love the Lord your God with all your heart, and with all your soul, and with all your mind.' This is the greatest and first commandment. And a second is like it: 'You shall love your neighbor as yourself.' On these two commandments hang all the law and the prophets.' " In the world of business, here lies the important lesson: We should treat our employees as we would treat ourselves.

8

BUILDING LONG-TERM RELATIONSHIPS

"I am the Alpha and the Omega," says the Lord God, who is and who was and who is to come, the Almighty.

—Revelation 1:8

Alpha and Omega, the first and last letters in the Greek alphabet, convey that our relationship with Jesus is forever.

Long-term relationships are essential in business; without them, success is only tentative. This applies to employees, customers, and vendors. Every businessperson knows that turnover of employees is expensive, because recruiting and training new people requires an investment of both money and time. Note too that experienced employees are more productive. Likewise, there are one-time costs to secure a new customer, but satisfied customers place larger orders next time. The same is true with vendors–over time, certain economies are realized through repeat business with the same companies. When we trust and feel comfortable with those we deal with, our business enjoys increased compatibility and harmony.

Of course, compatibility and harmony don't just happen. They take time to develop. A long-term relationship with deep roots can't help but blossom. You must have patience. Jesus clearly explains this required patience in Mark 4:3–8: "A sower went out to sow. And as he sowed, some seed fell on the path, and the birds came and ate it up. Other seed fell on rocky ground, where it did not have much soil, and it sprang up quickly, since it had no depth of soil. And when the sun rose, it was scorched; and since it had no root, it withered away. Other seed fell among thorns, and the thorns grew up and choked it, and it yielded no grain. Other seed fell into good soil and brought forth grain, growing up and increasing and yielding thirty and sixty and a hundredfold." This parable illustrates how relationships take time. Here, Jesus maintains that many seeds can be sowed, but not all of the sower's efforts will bear fruit. Yet if he is persistent and plants enough seed, some of it will grow and eventually yield great results–thirty-, sixty- and even one hundredfold. We also learn here that when we do succeed in building a long-term relationship, the yield is substantial and we are abundantly rewarded.

However, in order for relationships to grow, both parties must have faith and trust in each other. Otherwise, like seed that falls on rocky ground, gets scorched in the hot sun, or is choked by thorns, a relationship will not thrive. The faith and trust people have in each other takes time to develop. Through day-in and day-out performance, people slowly grow more comfortable as others prove they are reliable and truthful.

On a recent trip to Florida with my twenty-four-year-old son, David, Jr., I introduced him to the CEO of Northern Trust, the prestigious Chicago banking firm. After our meeting with the banker, I explained to Junior that the relationship I have today with Northern Trust was one that evolved over a period of time, and today, based on mutual respect and trust, both the bank and I feel comfortable about doing business together.

"The same holds true with long-term relationships you first built during your school days," I told my son. Years ago, my wife and I had to make sacrifices to send both of our children to private schools in St. Louis. In addition to receiving a fine education, both of them formed friendships with many children from our city's most prominent families. "Those high school friends know you well, son," I said, "and over the years, those long-term relationships will be beneficial. You and your friends will help each other succeed in your independent careers. You will partner in various ventures and do business with some of them because you and they feel comfortable with one another. You have a history together that's a result of having sown seeds in one another's lives for a long time. The rewards of those years of sowing will come to bear much fruit."

Always remember, people are watching you. They may be your old school friends, employers, customers, vendors–and they are constantly evaluating you. They observe your every move, checking to see if you walk the walk. In time, each long-term relationship you have will be based on your integrity and performance. In our business, we are now bearing fruit from seeds we sowed over the years. Or, as it is said in business, we are receiving the dividends from our investments. Our employee turnover is minimal and, consequently, we have a well-seasoned workforce. We are receiving reorders from longtime customers–repeat orders significantly larger than first-time orders. Likewise, our satisfied vendors approach us with requests to partner with them on future ventures. And most rewarding, our employees, customers, and vendors are constantly referring people to us–the finest compliment of a long-term relationship.

I cherish the long-term relationships I have with the men and women who work side by side with me at WWT. None is better exemplified than my special relationship with Jim Kavanaugh, who joined the company in 1990 at age twenty-eight. Starting in sales, Jim was named CEO of our parent company, World Wide Technology Holding Company, in early 2003. In addition to his title, Jim has an equity position in the company. Early on, based on his leadership and numerous contributions to the business, we talked about his future role in the company. On a handshake we agreed that he would someday have ownership in the company. Having explicit trust in each other, he knew that I would give him what he was due, and I knew he would do whatever it took to continue earning it.

In an entirely different arena, our company is committed to serve our community. Our people are encouraged to take an active leadership role in civic organizations–and they do so willingly because, after all, this is where we live and work. We support such groups as United Way, Ronald McDonald House, the Boy Scouts of America, local school boards, and many more. These too are important relationships to build, and the seeds we sow in these fields also bear delicious fruits.

9

TAKING A STAND

If the world hates you, be aware that it hated me before it hated you. If you belonged to the world, the world would love you as its own. Because you do not belong to the world, but I have chosen you out of the world—therefore the world hates you.

—John 15:18–19

Our nation has a rich heritage of great Americans who risked their lives to stand up for their beliefs. Imagine the courage required by those brave patriots who signed our nation's Declaration of Independence in 1776. To pick up a quill pen to sign that cherished document was an act of high treason against the British, equivalent to signing your own death warrant. This threat of execution prompted Benjamin Franklin to quip, "We must all hang together, or most assuredly we shall hang separately."

At the signing, Stephen Hopkins, a Rhode Island delegate who suffered from palsy, stalwartly said of his shaky signature, "My hand trembles, but my heart does not." And John Hancock defiantly wrote his name larger than any other signer to assure that the King of England could read it without his spectacles. What bravery these men displayed, knowing full well that the British had dispatched 32,000 fully equipped, highly trained professional British and Hessian (German) soldiers to our shores to halt the revolution. The British armada of 130 warships transporting these troops was an awesome military force, and the world's most powerful. In opposition, the colonies had an army of an estimated 9,000 poorly equipped amateur recruits. The colonists' navy–if it could be called a navy–didn't have a single available warship or transport. Against all odds, the Americans took a stand against a formidable enemy in a do-or-die fight for their freedom.

Throughout our rich history, there have been many brave Americans. One such woman who stood up for her beliefs was Harriet Tubman. She led an estimated three hundred African-Americans out of slavery in the South during the Civil War by making nineteen trips via the Underground Railroad, leading slaves to the North. Under her direction, once the slaves left their masters, there was no turning back. Those who became fearful and tried to retreat were told by the shotgun-toting Tubman, "Live North or die here." If the fugitives were caught, the consequences were torture and death.

Martin Luther King, Jr., the most acclaimed U.S. civil rights leader of the twentieth century, was at the forefront of the Civil Rights movement in the 1950s and 1960s. Known for his nonviolent political action, King never backed down in taking a stand for his beliefs. As a consequence, he and his family were in constant danger; in January 1956, his home was bombed. His activities in organizing and attending civil rights demonstrations meant he continually faced violence, beatings, and arrests. In 1968, he sought a coalition of black and white people to participate in a Poor People's March on Washington. The coalition was a move to broaden the Civil Rights movement to include the goals of economic justice and ending the Vietnam War. Prior to the march, he stopped in Memphis to help striking sanitation workers, and it was there on April 4, 1968, that James Earl Ray assassinated him. Martin Luther King took a stand for equal rights for African-Americans and he was victorious. It cost him his life. Courageous men and women such as Harriet Tubman and Martin Luther King, Jr., led the way for other Americans to follow in the fight against racial injustices in America.

When I was a small boy, my father used to tell stories about his days in the navy during World War II, when segregationists tried to keep him and other African-American sailors off their ship. On board, they were forced to eat at separate dining tables and sleep in separate quarters. There they were, putting their lives on the line for their country, and they were affronted by malicious indignities. They tolerated this abuse rather than cause dissension in the military. As my father explained to me, they were cognizant that there was a much bigger war to fight–America had a mission to defeat the Nazis.

Growing up in Clinton, Missouri, I remember dealing with the degradation of segregation. My older brothers and sisters went to Lincoln School, an all-black school with only two teachers–and that was for grades one through twelve. Even though it was a public school and African-Americans paid taxes like everyone else, Lincoln School students received hand-me-down books–leftovers from the white school on the other side of town. Lincoln's dilapidated building presented a striking contrast to the town's school for whites. Lincoln School was fully incorporated into the Clinton public school system in 1957. That year two African-American girls and I were enrolled in first grade. One of those girls, Anita Brame, and I continued through Clinton Middle School and then Clinton High School, going on to be the first African-Americans to go through the entire Clinton school system and graduate. As a young boy, I thought that in a small way, I too was making it easier for other African-American boys and girls who would someday attend integrated schools.

When I was sixteen, I was among a handful of African-American high-school students who integrated the public swimming pool in Clinton. There was a lot of racial hatred back in 1967, so there was no way of knowing what dire consequences we might face. Still, we did it, because we wanted to take a stand against segregation. God was on our side and there were no repercussions. From that day forward, the Clinton public swimming pool was integrated.

Growing up during the time that I did, I was subject to segregation at an early age and I also went through the transition that occurred during the beginning stages of integration. These experiences had a profound effect on the man I am today. I am not one to back down when it comes to taking a stand for what I believe. Sure, I know there are times when it's easier to turn my head and go along with the crowd–but that's not who I am.

While significant progress has occurred since my boyhood in curing the wrongs of racial bigotry, there are still subtle pockets of resistance. For instance, I sometimes feel indignation from some people who think that because I'm African-American, I don't belong in the information technology industry at my present capacity. Even here in the St. Louis area, some people resent seeing my wife and me hold responsible positions as board members of several civic and community organizations. In their minds, what we do deviates from what African-Americans traditionally do–and they don't like it. Like it or not, we are not about to stop doing what we believe is right. Thelma and I intend to become even more involved in these activities so we may serve as role models for others to follow in our footsteps.

The life of Jesus exemplifies the resolution to persist in one's beliefs. He knew his beliefs would be viewed as radical and that there would be enormous resistance, but that did not deter him from his mission. In John 15:18–19, Jesus says, "If the world hates you, be aware that it hated me before it hated you. If you belonged to the world, the world would love you as its own. Because you do not belong to the world, but I have chosen you out of the world–therefore the world hates you." The thought that there was hatred toward Jesus, the epitome of love and goodness, substantiates my belief that every one of us risks being subjected to opposition when we stand up for what is right. But no matter how strongly we are opposed, we should not back down. When I started out on my own, I knew the road would be bumpy and filled with obstacles. I knew that it would never be possible to satisfy everybody–so I don't try to. Instead, I do what's right, and I won't conform to satisfy others, knowing in my heart I am doing what is right.

10

CONSISTENCY

Now faith is the assurance of things hoped for, the conviction of things not seen.

—Hebrews 11:1

The central theme of the passage quoted above has significantly contributed to our company's success. I live my life consistently walking in faith knowing that God will do all he promises. To quote Great Britain's famous nineteenth-century prime minister Benjamin Disraeli: "The secret of success is consistency to purpose." The message of consistency to purpose is continually communicated to our entire organization. Consequently, every employee knows our singular purpose: to focus on excellence in every way we serve our customers. Just as Jesus had a singular purpose–to spread the Good News–we, too, have a commitment.

From the start, I told our people that we would always strive for excellence. This message was routinely repeated, and in time, everyone knew this as our mission. It's my opinion that employees want to believe in their management. They want to believe management will stand behind what it says. It goes beyond the spoken word. When we talk about excellence and quality, there are no compromises. Never. Only one standard is acceptable. It can never vary.

There will always be a temptation to relax one's standard for the sake of convenience. For instance, a time may come when an order must be shipped to satisfy an anxious customer, and someone will say, "Okay, let's push it out the door this one time. It's no big deal if it's not up to our standard work. It's a rush order and chances are, the customer won't even notice."

The customer might not know the difference, but your people will. Once they realize you have more than one standard, they'll think striving for excellence depends on management's mood at the time. It may not seem like much, but you've lost something: You've communicated to your people that quality isn't as important as you once led them to believe. They get confused. Now they think your lofty goal about excellence was just so much talk.

Quite simply, there has to be consistency. Look at the great companies in this world that succeed because they are consistent. McDonald's, for instance, trains teenagers at all its restaurants to turn out identical french fries and hamburgers. Those kids have parents at home who can't even get them to clean up their rooms, but McDonald's has them working its system to assure consistency to its customers. McDonald's consumers know exactly what to expect every time they visit and that's why they keep coming back.

Consistency is what drives people to purchase brand-name products. They know what they'll receive. They don't want surprises. Consistency is the secret behind chain hotels like Holiday Inn; travelers are assured every room will have the same level of quality. It's the same thing when you shop at the grocery store: You buy a specific brand-name product because you feel comfortable with the manufacturer's reputation, and that's why you buy the specific toothpaste you do–and soap and shoes and shirts.

Branding is about trust. You trust a particular manufacturer to turn out a product that you know meets a certain standard, time after time. Great brand companies establish a reputation in the marketplace, and their customers like knowing they'll receive the same consistent quality. They know what they'll get when they buy a pizza at Pizza Hut, stay at a Four Seasons hotel, or rent a car from Enterprise. And they trust these companies to deliver their products and services based on their reputations.

It's been said it takes a lifetime to build a good reputation, but it can be lost overnight. With this thought in mind, you must cherish your reputation and never take it for granted. For example, Arthur Andersen, a worldwide public accounting firm, enjoyed an impeccable reputation for 150 years, but lost it in a matter of days when it was publicly announced that a few of its high-level executives were found guilty of auditing improprieties with the firm's Enron account.

In *The NRSV Holy Bible*, the definition of a steward is: "A manager of a household or of property; used of Christians, particularly ministers, as guardians of the affairs of God." My wife and I like to tell people, "We are Stewards, and we have a responsibility to serve others." While this is said with a wink and a grin, we are earnest about being trustworthy, and we take very seriously what is said in 1 Corinthians 4:1–2, that we serve as stewards to Christ and God. The Scriptures also remind us that stewards are trustworthy.

Trust is the most important ingredient in building strong relationships. You earn the trust of others by being consistently honest in your dealings with them. In business, it starts internally–with your own people. Over time, you gain their trust because you treat them with fairness and respect. In time, they observe your single-minded focus on quality and how you serve your customers through delivering excellence in every transaction. They develop faith in you because they know you never deviate from doing the right thing. You do right with such consistency that they expect it–and you never disappoint them. This axiomatic value permeates the organization and is passed along to vendors and customers. It's a process–continual, nonstop.

11

TEAMWORK

Two are better than one, because they have a good reward for their toil. For if they fall, one will lift up the other; but woe to one who is alone and falls and does not have another to help. Again, if two lie together, they keep warm; but how can one keep warm alone? And though one might prevail against another, two will withstand one. A threefold cord is not quickly broken.

—Ecclesiastes 4:9–12

Paraphrasing the last sentence in this scripture, I often say, "The more strands it has, the stronger the rope." In the world of business, a team of people gains strength because everyone exerts effort. At World Wide Technology when many specialists work together as a team with a singular focus, each making a specific contribution, the company is able to realize significant synergy. To solve a particular problem for a customer, for example, we incorporate talents of our people from different areas such as operations, sales, accounting, distribution, and warehousing. This combined effort produces otherwise unattainable results. Of course, it helps when the people working in unison are exceptionally talented. And, much like a winning professional sports team, we're continually seeking the most talented people.

Our team development program cross-trains people to understand their coworkers' jobs. In football, that would be like an offensive lineman learning the quarterback's position and vice versa. The result is a better execution of plays, fewer turnovers, and so on. Likewise, it is advantageous for a finance person to understand other company areas like marketing and distribution, and so on.

The examples above illustrate how we apply teamwork within our company. Externally, we team up with vendors, and here too, the combined efforts can produce exceptional results. We apply the same principles of teamwork we use internally. When we pool our talents, and a vendor's people exert the same effort, we're able to accomplish more for the mutual benefit of both companies than had each worked independently. For example, Sun Microsystems is one of our vendors; we use their software and showcase it to mutual customers. We have similar partnerships with such companies as Dell, Cisco, and Oracle.

A word of caution: Not everyone wants to be a team player. Some people have their own agenda, one that doesn't jell with team objectives. For instance, in basketball, a poor team player is referred to as a "gunner"–someone who selfishly attempts poor shots rather than passing the ball to a teammate. In the Bible, an example of an infamous poor team player, who informed against Jesus, appears in Matthew 26:14–16. Judas Iscariot, one of the twelve disciples, betrayed Jesus by accepting thirty pieces of silver from the chief priests.

Like most companies, we've experienced our share of betrayals. What's interesting about teamwork is that other members of the team tend to weed out poor team players. Rarely do we fire anyone–instead the non-team player will quit after being rejected by other team players. These individuals stick out like a sore thumb.

When it becomes evident they lack single-mindedness of purpose, it's practically impossible for them to fit in. No, we're not shy about firing a non–team player, and we don't hesitate when that's necessary, but in most cases, they leave of their own accord.

In John 15:1–2, Jesus uses a parable about how his Father is a vine grower who removes all branches that bear no fruit, and how each branch that does bear fruit is pruned to make it bear even more fruit. Likewise, we prune in the workplace where it is necessary to let strong players replace weak players until everyone works in unison.

12

RISK-TAKING

Blessed are those who have not seen and yet have come to believe.

—John 20:29

In the passage above, Jesus could very well have been addressing a business leadership convention with this message. Although a decision-maker believes he will achieve positive results from time and money invested in a business venture, the outcome is not guaranteed. One thing we do know: No one of this world is capable of predicting the future with absolute accuracy.

In 1609, the first colonists were dispatched to the New Land to form the Jamestown colony. Lotteries were conducted to determine who would settle in the faraway, uncivilized land. The colonies were actually set up as little corporations to profit London shareholders, who, in their own right, were risk-takers.

Due to sickness, starvation, and hostile Indians, during its first winter in 1610 the Jamestown settlement of five hundred people dropped to only sixty. Still, more and more settlers came to America, crossing treacherous waters to reach their destination. Years later, brave men and women pioneered across the Great Plains, in covered wagons and on horseback, then later by train, traveling through hostile territory. American history is filled with great risk-taking adventurers: the forty-niners who rushed to California in search of gold; the early riders of the Pony Express; the Texans who struck oil at Spindletop, an oil field whose first-year output doubled that of Russia, then the world's number-one petroleum producer. The list of our nation's risk-takers is still growing. Today, millions of Americans each year invest their life savings and incur great debt to start their own businesses. We are truly a nation of risk-takers.

Risks are taken by men and women who are not satisfied with the status quo. Of course, there are many more discontented people who settle for less because they are uncomfortable with change and won't take risks. Why? Because change represents the unknown. They have not seen the future, and feel that if change occurs, it might not be to their benefit.

Successful businesspeople take risks commensurate with what they feel they will receive in return. Simply put, the greater the risk, the greater the opportunity for high profits. For example, an offshore oil company will invest large sums of money in exploration of petroleum with, say, ten-to-one odds of discovery. But, with possible returns far greater than ten to one, the company takes even more risk. To hedge its bets, the oil company will seek opportunities to drill enough wells so their chances of success become favorable. So while a majority of wells are likely to be dry holes, the return on investment of the one that hits will generate more than enough profit to compensate for the unsuccessful wells. For instance, with ten-to-one odds against striking oil, but with a fifteen-to-one return on investment for a successful well, there is sufficient incentive for risk-taking.

The Bible encourages risk-taking, as Jesus illustrates in the Parable of the Talents, which appears in Matthew 25:14–30. Here, Jesus tells of a wealthy man, who, before leaving on a journey, summoned three of his slaves to come forth. He gave five talents to one slave, two talents to a second slave, and one talent to a less worthy slave. Upon his departure, the slave with five talents went off at once and traded with them, and made five more talents. The second man who had the two talents did the same and he made two more talents. But the third man with a single talent dug a hole in the ground and hid his master's money. When the master of the slaves returned, he beckoned them to come forth to see what they did with their money.

The first slave said, "Master, you handed over to me five talents and see, I have made five more talents." The master replied, "Well done, good and trustworthy slave. You have done well so I will put you in charge of many things." The slave with the two talents also explained how he had earned two more talents, and he too had pleased the master. The master also gave him more responsibility.

The slave who had received one talent came forth and said, "Master, I knew that you were a harsh man, reaping where you did not sow, and gathering where you did not scatter seed; so I was afraid, and I went and hid your talent in the ground. Here you have what is yours." To him, the master replied, "You wicked and lazy slave! You knew, did you, that I reap where I did not sow, and gather where I did not scatter? Then you ought to have invested my money with the bankers, and on my return I would have received what was my own with interest." The master then took the one talent from him and gave it to the first slave to add to his ten talents. The master declared, "For to all those who have more, more will be given, and they will have an abundance; but from those who have nothing, even what they have will be taken away. As for this worthless slave, throw him into the outer darkness, where there will be weeping and gnashing of teeth."

In the above parable, the slave who simply buried his money eliminated any possible opportunity for profit. Hence, his master ostracized him for being irresponsible. As Jesus teaches, we should not shy away from opportunity, nor the risk that accompanies it. In baseball parlance, it's called "swinging for the fence." Note for example, that Babe Ruth had 714 career home runs–he also struck out 1,330 times, a major league record. And Thomas Edison, one of the world's greatest inventors, recorded 25,000 failures in his attempt to invent a storage battery. When interviewed about his work on the shortage battery, Edison replied, "Those were not failures. I just learned 25,000 ways not to make a storage battery."

I believe the Lord measures us by how many times we get up, not by how many times we fail. Babe Ruth is immortalized for the number of home runs he hit, not the number of times he struck out. And Edison is remembered for the number of successful inventions he had–and there were many. The U.S. Patent and Trademark Office granted 1,093 patents to Edison, far more than to any other individual.

Due to the nature of the technology industry, I am in a high-risk business. It is a capital-intensive business, requiring large investments of money well in advance of any chance for profit. With continual change in technology, equipment and software can quickly become obsolete, so the window of opportunity for a company to get an adequate return on its investment can be small.

I credit my mother for instilling in me the belief that I would succeed if I tried hard enough and refused to give in to failure. "You have to take that leap of faith, David," I can still hear her telling me. I've passed this inheritance along to my children, and I know they both aspire to take that leap of faith to do something with their lives that will make a difference. And I have been blessed to have a supportive wife who has faith that God is working his vision through me. True, there will be setbacks along the way–if not, it wouldn't be called risk-taking. Risk-takers encounter setbacks along the way but don't permit that to defeat them. Instead, they learn from their mistakes and grow stronger, never doubting they will eventually succeed.

As I look back at the challenges and setbacks Thelma and I along with our staff faced during the early years of this company, I can see we learned much from those hard times. What's more, if we didn't experience the difficulties we had to endure, we wouldn't be the strong company we are today. "You can't skip steps," I tell our people. "It's a process."

I may have founded the company, but by no means was I the only risk-taker at WWT. The first employees also took risks when they left their jobs at established companies to work for a brand-new business, one that was operated by an African-American with no prior entrepreneurial experience. Jim Kavanaugh, for instance, was a sales rep for Future Electronics, a $400 million company headquartered in Montreal. Leaving his job to come to work for a small start-up company that began on a shoestring required considerable faith.

While attending St. Louis University, Jim traveled with the United States Olympic Soccer Team for eighteen months. Back in the early 1990s, it was unusual for a young white male to join an

African-American–owned company. When Jim was recently asked if this caused him to ever have second thoughts about joining WWT, he replied, "Not at all. I was blessed to have the good fortune to travel around the world and play soccer with individuals from many different cultures. Consequently, I learned that the color of one's skin has no bearing on an individual's performance–on or off the soccer field. I judge a person by his character, not by the color of his skin." I was blessed to have people like Jim believe in me, especially when many people were predicting that it was only a matter of time before WWT would go belly-up.

I am inspired by the words in 2 Timothy 4:7–8: "I have fought the good fight, I have finished the race, I have kept the faith. From now on there is reserved for me the crown of righteousness, which the Lord, the righteous judge, will give me on that day, and not only to me but also to all who have longed for his appearing." This passage assures me I can take risks and keep my faith; I shall not only persevere, I shall succeed.

13

BEING A CUSTOMER-DRIVEN COMPANY

In everything do to others as you would have them do to you.

—Matthew 7:12

Known as the Golden Rule, this is perhaps the most quoted scripture in the Bible, and as far as I'm concerned, no one has ever come up with a better philosophy about how to treat people. It works with everyone–employees and customers alike. It's what we do at World Wide Technology. A Golden Rule attitude is deeply ingrained in our corporate culture, and it permeates our relationships with customers and vendors.

With a constant focus on our customers, every employee is treated as if he or she were a customer. Here's how it works: Different people within our organization are customers to other people from other areas of the organization. For instance, marketing people are the accounting people's customers; distribution people are the marketing people's customers. And support teams in various departments have their own customers within their own departments, and so on. In my position as CEO, every company employee is my customer. I repeat: Good leadership makes a priority of serving the people within an organization.

With the focus always on customers, every employee has a clear understanding of how his or her job relates to customers. And I mean everyone, from the receptionist at the front desk to the dock loader in the shipping area. This also applies to an employee who has no direct contact with a customer: What he or she does is still relevant to serving customers. That's because the *entire* company exists to serve customers.

On any given day, you're apt to see customers and vendors visiting our facilities. They're invited to tour our operation and meet our people. We encourage them to come get a feel for our culture. Browsing around, they witness a working environment filled with excitement—they see firsthand an organization that thrives on serving customers. There are no closed doors, and that includes mine. It's always open to employees, customers, and vendors.

We are particularly pleased with the partnerships we have with vendors. This is a major part of our business, and we're delighted to engage in joint ventures with them. We're aware that they could easily have selected one of our competitors, and we feel honored because companies partner with people they care about and trust. I view these partnerships as cherished relationships. When we form an agreement with another company, I pray and ask God to bless the union. I ask him to bless the coming together of both parties and ask that it be profitable for both sides. A business deal can never be successful if it's one-sided. When that happens, everyone loses.

We view each of our employees as a company ambassador.

Not many companies share this point of view, but to us, it's imperative. There are times when a particular employee is the only personal contact a customer has with the company, and when that happens, he or she represents the entire company. Wal-Mart, the world's largest company with sales in 2001 in excess of $217 billion, has more than 4,100 stores and 1.2 million employees. To continue the friendliness that its late founder, Sam Walton, extended when he personally served customers in his first store, each Wal-Mart store has a "greeter," who welcomes shoppers at the door. In addition to offering a friendly welcome, the greeter directs people who need directions to find merchandise in the store. The greeter and the cashier may be the customer's only personal contact with a Wal-Mart employee, in which case these two important employees are Wal-Mart ambassadors who represent the entire 1.2 million-employee workforce.

Likewise, a field rep who handles a customer's account may represent the entire company. In a large multibillion-dollar insurance company such as Metropolitan Life, the agent is often the only MetLife employee the customer meets. With this in mind, a customer often bases his image of the company on his impression of this single agent. The same is true regarding the impression made by a receptionist on a first-time visitor. It takes only a single unfriendly reception to make a customer think, "Boy, what a cold place. I'll never come back here again."

One of Thelma's and my favorite restaurants in St. Louis is Tony's. It has a five-star rating for its fine food, but we appreciate the exceptional service even more. The owner, Vince Bommarito, always welcomes us with a warm greeting: "Mr. and Mrs. Steward, it is such a pleasure to see you." Or, if we haven't been there for a while, he'll say, "Mr. and Mrs. Steward, we miss seeing you." On special occasions such as a birthday or anniversary, Vince will send roses or a dessert to our table.

There's something very special when the owner of a business personally greets you. It's as if the entire company is welcoming you or thanking you for your patronage. Nobody else can do this quite as well as the owner. Knowing how my wife and I personally feel when Vince showers us with attention, I work hard to make our customers feel appreciated in a similar way. For this reason, I'm constantly visiting major customers and vendors, letting them know how much we appreciate their business. I frequently criss-cross the country so I can be in front of CEOs and management. My job is to reassure them that we care about them. I want them to know that if they have any concerns or questions about our company–or any suggestions for improvement–they can come directly to me. We never take them for granted, no matter how close a relationship we might have developed with them over the years. We never want to become complacent about it. In fact, the bigger we grow, the more we are aware that the competition is ready to step into our place if we falter.

Paul offers some excellent advice in 2 Corinthians 9:6–11 when he says that an individual who sows sparingly will also reap sparingly; likewise, someone who sows bountifully will also reap bountifully. Paul also reminds us that God loves a cheerful giver, and he will provide abundantly for a person who shares abundantly in every good work. This scripture reminds us to serve others because we care about them, not because there is profit to be made. This is how I feel about our customers. I willingly serve them without thought of profit. Over time, I believe customers recognize this form of sincere caring, and consequently, a special relationship evolves. Ultimately, this is what builds great customer loyalty.

The rewards from loyal customers are manifold. In addition to giving you repeat orders that are bigger than initial orders, they refer other customers to you. And remember too that satisfied customers become your best salespeople. To paraphrase what Jesus said in Mark 4:8, when seed is planted in good soil, it has a high yield. This has been my company's experience–the sowing of seed with customers has multiplied our business thirty-, fifty-, and one hundredfold.

14

CONFRONTATION

The eye is the lamp of the body. So, if your eye is healthy, your whole body will be full of light, but if your eye is unhealthy, your whole body will be full of darkness. If then the light in you is darkness, how great is the darkness!

—Matthew 6:22–23

In the above scripture, Jesus says to be open to opposing viewpoints. Throughout the Bible, there are many instances of confrontation. But we must be tolerant and recognize that confrontation is not necessarily negative. For example, in Exodus 3:16–17, Moses is instructed by God to speak to the elders of Israel and inform them of his meeting at the burning bush. Here, Moses is told to announce that God has chosen him to lead the Israelites out of Egypt and to the land of milk and honey.

After the eighty-year-old Moses listens to his marching orders, he reluctantly pleads with God to choose somebody else because the people may not believe or listen to him. Moses claims that he lacks leadership skills. He asks God to choose someone who doesn't stutter. Nonetheless, God insists that Moses must obey his wishes.

Moses was also weary of confronting the Pharaoh–the King of Egypt and arguably the most powerful man of his day. The Pharaoh was considered so mighty his people worshipped him as a god.

Imagine the modest Moses–a stutterer–being selected to confront such an overbearing individual–a vain, proud dictator with a giant-sized ego. Moses' first meeting with the Pharaoh wasn't his last. Again and again, he pleaded his case with the Pharaoh, at each encounter warning of an impending catastrophe to be inflicted on the Egyptians if the Pharaoh refused to let his people go. The forecasted calamities included plague, famine, swarming locusts, and death to every Egyptian family's first-born male. Presenting such a horrendous array of ultimatums to a Pharaoh was fraught with peril. Although Moses was by no means an enthusiastic volunteer for the post, he accepted the assignment and dutifully served. His strong faith in God was indeed uncompromising.

Jesus also faced continual confrontation–bear in mind that most people did not accept him as the Messiah. Mark 11:15–18 describes an encounter Jesus had while spreading the Word upon coming to Jerusalem. Jesus went to the temple and was appalled to see merchants and money changers conducting business within its hallowed walls. Enraged, Jesus turned over tables and shouted that what was a house of prayer had become a den of robbers. Feeling threatened by his dissension, the chief priests and the scribes opposed Jesus. Their confrontation could have caused Jesus to be stoned. Nonetheless, his conviction in his beliefs never wavered.

Like Moses and Jesus, but on a lesser scale, many times we must remain faithful to our beliefs despite confrontation. When a valued employee steps out of line or a customer violates our principles, we must confront them. Here, I again emphasize the importance of demonstrating qualities like trust, integrity, commitment, and loyalty. I stand for these. In matters of principle, there is no margin for compromise. As a manager, I know people are constantly watching me to evaluate my position on issues. If I should waver, employees would question whether to place their careers and their family's welfare in my hands; they would doubt their opportunities for growth and development under my leadership. These feelings could cause them to look elsewhere for stability. To effectively lead others, I must stand fast, and believe me, it's not always the easy thing to do. Sometimes employees test me, much as children do a parent, to see if my position is firm. As we all know, it's easier to do what's popular. But to go with the flow–to do what will please the majority–may not be the right thing to do. Remember: You're running a company, not participating in a popularity contest.

The examples of Moses and Jesus above illustrate confrontation facing strong opposition. We too face daily incidences, however mild, in comparison: a rude remark, a discourteous driver, a disagreeable store clerk. On the other hand, severe confrontation can mean political upheaval or even war. In business, confrontation can surface when there are opposing views. Many people view confrontation as undesirable in the workplace; they see every conflict as a growing source of dissention and a destroyer of teamwork. People who are frequently confrontational are labeled "troublemakers." Hence, to most, confrontation has a negative undertone.

A delicate balance, however, should be maintained so that confrontation in the workplace is permitted and even encouraged. That's because permitting people to present opposing views has a positive value. By "delicate balance," I am implying *some* confrontation is good–to a certain point. At World Wide Technology, everyone is encouraged to speak out and challenge the status quo. It would be foolish to try to stifle open debate. We want people to feel comfortable opposing commonly accepted views, rather than feel too intimidated to express their points of view. This is not to suggest we condone out-of-control confrontation, shouting matches, or pitting people against others in the organization.

In business, it's essential to listen to differing opinions with an open mind. Jesus explained this in Matthew 7:1–5: "Do not judge, so that you may not be judged. For with the judgment you make you will be judged, and the measure you give will be the measure you get. Why do you see the speck in your neighbor's eye, but do not notice the log in your own eye? Or how can you say to your neighbor, 'Let me take the speck out of your eye,' while the log is in your own eye? You hypocrite, first take the log out of your own eye, and then you will see clearly to take the speck out of your neighbor's eye." What valuable advice. Often, we approach a different viewpoint in a confrontational way so quickly that we miss the real message: Something else may actually be preferable to our own position. If someone confronts us, we shouldn't let defensiveness blind us to a fatal flaw in our position.

Having a sales and marketing background, I approach business differently than Jim Kavanaugh, who approaches business from an operations point of view. Consequently, the skill set I bring to the table is much different from his. I am an entrepreneur, and as Jim puts it, "the consummate risk-taker." He, on the other hand, is a disciplined manager with a financial perspective. Hence, there are areas where he is strong and I am weak, and vice versa. As a result, we complement each other. Do our differences sometimes result in confrontation? Definitely. At the same time, our differences provide a healthy balance that has significantly contributed to the company's overall success. Jim has never been shy about expressing his views, and when he disagrees with me, he is quick to challenge me. I know he does it with the company's best interests in mind, and I welcome it.

It is true that some organizations are quick to nip any form of confrontation in the bud and eliminate it by decree of an iron-fisted boss. No one dares to front any opposition. Consequently, such bosses are surrounded by yes-men, and rarely get an honest opinion. They like the fact that everybody expresses the same opinion–theirs! We all know the fallacies of this dictatorship style of management. It simply doesn't permit employees to think on their own. When creativity is discouraged, how can staff take pride in their work? Only a person with a big ego refuses to respect the opinions of others. As far as I'm concerned, ego is an acronym for "edging God out." Conversely, when leaders care about people, they humbly listen to them, knowing their opinions have value. It's equally important that their people *know* they're being listened to.

Unfortunately, egos run rampant in corporate America, and surface mostly in the higher echelons–the farther up the corporate ladder you go, the more likely you are to encounter executives with egos that get in their way and work against them. Individuals who think too highly of themselves turn a deaf ear to opposing views. So while they may stifle the voice of confrontation, shutting the door on innovation and creativity exacts a high price.

I believe strong leadership encourages people to express opposing views. This requires managers to set aside their pride and willingly permit people to find holes in their position. When managers foster out-of-the-box thinking, their people rise to the challenge. The key is to create a relaxed environment void of bureaucracy. Just how this works can be seen in our conference room. The room has a large conference table; however, anyone, regardless of rank, can sit at the head of the table. I rarely do. Every seat is as important as any other. When I sit elbow to elbow with my employees on either side of me, that says, "We're all in this together."

15

HAVING A VISION

But strive first for the kingdom of God and his righteousness, and all these things will be given to you as well.

—Matthew 6:33

I recently heard about a CEO of a troubled company who was lost at sea on a solo sailing trip. While gazing at the stars, he had a vision of where to lead his organization. When the inspired CEO was rescued, he returned to his company headquarters and met with his management team to proclaim his vision. Consequently, they rallied around him and the company made an amazing turnaround. It worked, so I'm not knocking it. Regardless of where or how his vision originated, it was effective because the CEO had come up with a game plan to guide his people to reach his clearly defined goal.

I strongly believe that to lead, one must have a vision. It's the vision that provides the leader and his organization with direction. The lack of a vision is akin to traveling across the country with no roadmap and no destination. As a result, you turn in this direction, then go that way, meandering everywhere. In your trip to nowhere, you wander aimlessly and end up lost.

Did you ever wake up on a Saturday morning with no plans for the entire day? Without an agenda, you drift through the entire day and nothing gets done. You read the newspaper, watch television, talk on the telephone–and before you know it, night comes. By the end of the day, you feel down because you wasted a day of your life, a precious day that can never be replaced. Just as you can drift through an entire day, some people drift through their entire lives without direction. Many businesses also aimlessly drift. The owner goes to work every day and makes a living but accomplishes very little. When it's all said and done, had that business never existed, it would not have mattered.

A clear vision, however, sets a course of action with direction. Once again, I'll say that a vision isn't something your subconscious mind dreams up in the middle of the night, or a brainstorm that causes a lightbulb to suddenly go off. A vision is a definite goal about what you want your company to be in the future. Serious thought must be given to it and then correspondingly sufficient time allowed for it to form. Bear in mind that a vision isn't about what you want to do for you; it's about what you can do to better serve people. For example, having a vision to own a multibillion-dollar company or become a multimillionaire is simply wishful thinking. But when you have a vision about how to benefit others–that's an entirely different story. When you fill a need for others, wealth follows. That's the reward, not the vision.

A classic example of a wish versus a vision is the story behind the 1957 Edsel, which began as a tribute to Henry Ford's son Edsel. Ford Motor Company wanted to produce a radically different automobile, and price it midway between the Mercury and the Lincoln–a slot dominated by General Motors. The Edsel was designed with controversial styling and innovative equipment, such as push-button transmission controls on the steering wheel, self-adjusting brakes, safety rim wheels, and a "horse-collar" grill. While the Edsel might have been the car Ford executives wanted to sell, it was clearly not what the American consumer wanted. As a consequence, the name Edsel has become synonymous with a blunder of epic proportions. Had Ford management's vision focused on a car to serve the needs of the consumer, the Edsel may have succeeded and the word "Edsel" would have an entirely different meaning today. Seven years later, in 1964, Ford introduced another car, but in a much different scenario. This time, the company had a vision of a moderately priced four-door sports car, one that marketing research showed would fill a need for the American consumer. Serving the customer's needs, the Mustang set a first-year sales record of over 400,000 cars, and profits exceeded $1 billion.

Regardless of the size of the business, every owner needs a vision to succeed. According to the Scriptures, this vision must be focused on serving others; a self-serving plan has no merit. Do what is right for others and you will be rewarded. As Jesus tells us in Matthew 6:33: "But strive first for the kingdom of God and his righteousness, and all these things will be given to you as well." Putting other people first and serving them means you no longer have to worry about yourself, because good things will automatically happen. This is why your vision should be all about sowing seed in other people's lives. In my business, it's never about me. I'm there to serve my people and give them the support they require so we can serve our customers and vendors. This plan gets me excited about coming to work each morning. And when I travel to visit our customers and vendors across the country, I take that opportunity to validate our commitment to serve them. I am there to let them know that they're dealing with a company where the customer's needs come first, where only by satisfying those needs is it possible for us to satisfy our own.

When a new customer or vendor agrees to do business with World Wide Technology, he becomes part of our overall vision of doing good for those we serve. During the initial stage of the relationship, we go through a getting-acquainted period. Over time, based on performance, a mutual trust develops. Due to the nature of our business, we make a sizeable investment in each new customer. To start the ball rolling, a lot of resources in terms of money, time, and energy must be invested up front. Later, when we finally send an invoice to a new customer, there's usually a thirty- to sixty-day period before a first payment is received. WWT must have faith and trust in our customer, or a strong relationship cannot evolve. Today, we have formed partnerships with many top Fortune 500 companies–and some accounts have grown into eight- and nine-figure annual transactions. Many began as small contracts that increased in size: By giving much to our customers, we receive much in return. Conversely, a company that offers little value to its customers will have its customers taken away by competitors that provide more.

At work, people frequently describe me as the optimist who insists the glass is half full. I concur; that's an accurate description. My mother instilled this optimism in my siblings and me when we were small, for which I am forever grateful. She taught us all things are possible, and this belief was reinforced in church every Sunday. As a child, I remember hearing members of the congregation say to me, "Little David, play on your harp." I liked being compared to David, one of my favorite biblical heroes. As a child,

I imagined myself, David's namesake, daring to do seemingly impossible things–I truly believed I someday would.

Later, when I played basketball, we learned to anticipate where the ball would be before it was there. Sure, that's a split-second vision, but nonetheless, it's thinking a step ahead. A member of a sports team succeeds by focusing on one play at a time, and a team becomes conference champion by winning one game at a time. When we were a small company, I had a big vision for the future, but I also realized to get there, we'd do it one step at a time.

In 1995, our annual revenues were $74 million. At the time, I announced to our people that we'd exceed the billion-dollar mark by 2003. I explained that it would happen by serving our customers and finding ways to improve the value we give them. Now, to make our vision happen, we committed ourselves to invest large sums of money into our e-business infrastructure. We also had to take our seed and sow it into technology and personnel. We could have opted to stuff our pockets, which some businesspeople do rather than continue to take extended risks. Their thinking is: "We've built this company to this point and taken very little out of it. Rather than risk what we now have, let's cash in while we can."

That kind of thinking isn't an option with us. We have a vision to build something extraordinary that will provide outstanding service for generations and generations. As far as we are concerned, we've just begun to spread our wings. It is true we have a grand vision. Our people know that we will continue to sacrifice and apply team effort until our long-term vision is realized.

By definition, leadership is leading people into the future. (Conversely, going backward into the past is not leading.) Good leaders clearly communicates their vision to followers. That way, they understand where they are headed. Although the future is not predictable, people feel secure being told the organization's plans and being included in those plans. Communication beats being left in the dark. Your people want to believe management has a strategy for the future; it gives them hope for a better tomorrow. After Moses relayed his vision of the Promised Land to his people, they wandered forty years in the wilderness until they found it. Had Moses not communicated his vision, it is unlikely the Israelites would have followed him. Likewise, in today's business world, a leader must articulate his vision to his people. At the very least, they will be energized. That's because they'll know where they're headed.

It helps a leader to feel certain his vision will someday happen. In my particular case, I knew it would. Going far back to when I was hiring my first people, I had total faith in my vision. I believed in it so strongly that when I interviewed prospective employees, many of them were able to sense my passion for our vision. If an interviewee didn't buy into it, he or she didn't come aboard. I realized not everyone would share my vision, and if they didn't, it didn't matter. I knew there'd be others who would.

When I knew God was within me, interestingly, others began to share my vision. Of course, even the most enthusiastic person can't be on a high all the time. Roadblocks along the way may be discouraging. I had my share of setbacks and, believe me, there were difficult times. During those periods, I rejuvenated my belief in my vision by repeating the words found in Isaiah 41:10: "Do not fear, for I am with you, do not be afraid, for I am your God; I will strengthen you, I will help you, I will uphold you with my victorious right hand." With God on my side, I knew I would succeed.

Finally, we must remember that having a vision is only a beginning. It furnishes you a roadmap, but you must still put strategies in place and develop tactics. Then you must run a good operation to implement your strategies and tactics. Remember too, realizing a vision is a process–it could be five years, ten years, or more into the future. As you near realization of your vision, it may evolve into something ever greater. Though it may seem a little out of reach, with God's help, it's always attainable.

16

LONG-TERM THINKING

They shall be like a tree planted by water, sending out its roots by the stream. It shall not fear when heat comes, and its leaves shall stay green; in the year of drought it is not anxious, and it does not cease to bear fruit.

—Jeremiah 17:8

Like a tree prudently planted by a stream so it may receive nourishment and grow strong, a business must base its plans on long-term growth so it can grow.

As a privately held corporation, World Wide Technology is not subject to pressures that the investment community exerts on management. This freedom allows us to focus on long-term investments so we can strengthen our infrastructure and be rewarded five, ten, and fifteen years from now. We make this investment today so our company can prosper many tomorrows from now. I believe this long-term thinking is in the best interests of our employees, customers, and vendors. The seeds we wisely sow today will be reaped a hundredfold in years to come.

When my company was in its infancy compared to what I envisioned it would someday be, I made a commitment that my style of management would be based on giving to others. I always believed that those who give also receive. I abided by this basic tenet early on, and it is the doctrine I live by today as CEO of a billion-dollar enterprise. It is true I have been richly rewarded, and for that I will be eternally grateful. The success and size of our organization has not altered my belief in giving to others. It has, however, broadened the scope of my ministry; I am gratified to have the opportunity to reach out to even more people.

Unquestionably, there were times when I had to make difficult decisions that required the company to sacrifice short-term profits in order to someday realize long-term gains. I won't kid you and say it was easy. Being able to generate short-term profits is tempting, especially for a start-up company in dire need of cash. But we refused to compromise our principles and we patiently bided our time, believing that we would someday be rewarded. As I said earlier, faith is believing in the unseen.

Speaking of patience, the story of Job is the Bible's classic on the subject. The Book of Job depicts how Satan challenged God to test the faith of Job, a righteous, religious man who was one of the richest men in the world. The devil insisted to God that Job was faithful to him only because he had been given so much. But if you took away all Job's wealth, Satan proposed, he would lose his faith. Accepting the challenge, God put Job in the hands of Satan. Thereupon, Job's property was destroyed, including all of his land and cattle. Later, the devil afflicted him with disease and killed his children. Still Job's faith remained resolute. His body covered with boils, Job was wracked with pain. At this point, even his wife denied God. When his friends told him he must have committed a terrible sin to be punished so severely, Job denied having sinned. Yet, he refused to curse God, even when he cried out against the injustice of his fate. All the while, Job continued to believe in and revere God.

Finally, God told Satan that Job had proven he was faithful and took him under his care again. He restored Job fully, providing him with twice what he previously had. So, while Job had endured enormous suffering and anguish, the Lord rewarded him with great wealth to enjoy for his remaining years. God also blessed Job with beautiful daughters, whose beauty surpassed all other women in the land. Job lived to the ripe old age of 140, and lived to see four generations of his children prosper. As the Scriptures read, Job died old and full of days.

The story of Job illustrates the patience a long-term thinker must have. Above all else, one must never abandon his or her faith in God, no matter how dire the circumstance. Job's tale teaches us to endure and not submit to our doubts–though there may be much doubt along the way. In Mark 11:22–25, Jesus says: "Have faith in God. Truly I tell you, if you say to this mountain, 'Be taken up and thrown into the sea,' and if you do not doubt in your heart, but believe that what you say will come to pass, it will be done for you. So I tell you, whatever you ask for in prayer, believe that you have received it, and it will be yours. Whenever you stand praying, forgive, if you have anything against anyone; so that your Father in heaven may also forgive you your trespasses." What powerful words of encouragement! Be aware, however, there is a stipulation in this message: When you ask God in prayer for his blessings, you must forgive others. These verses also tell us that though at times our doubts may look like mountains, with faith we shall overcome them. When you start a new business venture–perhaps on a shoestring like I did–your long-term objectives may appear so remote as to seem unattainable. Have faith. Again and again throughout the Scriptures we are told that all things are possible with Christ, who gives us strength.

Our doubts may cause concern because there is no guarantee we will realize our long-term plan. This is where strong faith in God is essential, because we never know in advance how long it will be before we succeed. While on your lengthy journey to fulfill your long-term plan, be careful not to submit to short-term temptations. You may be sure there will be many temptations along the way to distract you. There will also be distracters who urge you to give in to short-term gains. In a publicly held company, for example, investors and analysts exert pressure, demanding short-term gains to boost quarterly financial statements. Short-term investors' interests may be best served by a temporary increase in the price of a traded stock. A favorable announcement will enable them to sell their holdings and realize a quick profit. This type of investor is not concerned about the future of a company. Accordingly, this same investor resists long-term capital expenditures that decrease short-term profits but enhance the welfare of the company in years to come. As we are instructed in 1 Timothy 6:10, the love of money is a root of all kinds of evil, and in their eagerness to be rich, many people lose their faith.

17

A MISSION STATEMENT

Blessed are the poor in spirit, for theirs is the kingdom in heaven. Blessed are those who mourn, for they will be comforted. Blessed are the meek, for they will inherit the earth. Blessed are those who hunger and thirst for righteousness, for they will be filled. Blessed are the merciful, for they will receive mercy. Blessed are the pure in heart, for they will see God. Blessed are the peacemakers, for they will be called children of God. Blessed are those who are persecuted for righteousness sake, for theirs is the kingdom of heaven. Blessed are you when people revile you and persecute you and utter all kinds of evil against you falsely on my account. Rejoice and be glad, for your reward is great in heaven, for in the same way they persecuted the prophets who were before you.

—Matthew 5:3–12

Jesus' blessings, known as the Beatitudes, appear in his Sermon on the Mount and were told to his disciples. He spoke these words from his heart and they are similar to a mission statement.

Ideally, every company should have a mission statement in writing to convey its guiding principles to its people. Having said that, I'll admit relatively few start-up companies do. Many small entrepreneurs are not current on the most recent management books promoting mission statements. Their daily trials and tribulations keep them too busy fighting for survival to commit what they stand for to paper.

Coming from corporate America, I'd been exposed to many mission statements, so I was one of those uncommon start-up company owners who actually had one. It was plainly stated and right to the point. It read: "*People*, *quality*, and *technology*."

From the start, I focused on getting the best people and treating them right as my top priority. Customers and vendors were included. Then I made it very clear to everyone that the company was dedicated to providing the highest level of quality to our customers. I also emphasized we would deliver exceptional service to our customers and vendors via state-of-the-art technology. Technology would also be utilized internally as a tool to serve employees.

We were looking for top people in a highly competitive environment, and back then we didn't have the wherewithal to pay top-dollar salaries. For an infant company, a mission statement was an excellent way to announce to the world what we stood for. In this respect, it helped us attract the best people because it articulated our values. Even though we were a brand-new company, people came aboard because we had faith in what we were doing and our enthusiasm was contagious. While our original mission statement has evolved into something different today, one reason it worked was its clarity and brevity. Those qualities are just as important today. I believe the best mission statements are easily understood as well as easy to remember. What's the point of having a confusing mission statement or one that's hard to remember?

Anyone searching for a mission statement that can be applied in business as well as in all walks of life might consider the Golden Rule. Many companies have adopted this doctrine as their mission statement. Another gem appears in Mark 12:31: "You shall love your neighbor as yourself." Both of these verses–simple, yet eloquently put–can serve as guiding principles for people in any organization on how to conduct their daily business practices. As an added bonus, because each is a brief sentence, they are easily remembered. I like a mission statement that can be committed to memory. I figure, easy to quote, easy to follow.

Our company's mission statement has altered over the years, and today it reads: "Provide a revolutionary way to streamline and simplify the global IT supply chain, all from a single source–WWT." Admittedly, it's a little longer, but still can be quoted verbatim.

Our guiding principles are:

Embrace change.
Honesty and integrity first.
Promote a positive attitude.
Move fast, never procrastinate.
Be creative, take chances, make mistakes.
Always give your best and be a team player.
Be passionate about what you do or do something else.
Be loyal to yourself, your family, and your fellow employees.
Understand, embrace, and integrate yourself into the world of e-business.

Admittedly, our guiding principles are too lengthy for most people to remember without effort. To create awareness for both our mission statement and guiding principles, they are prominently displayed on posters throughout every one of our buildings, and you will also find them on our website.

Mission statements and guiding principles remind people what you stand for. However, I offer a word of caution: Be sure to practice what you preach. Making claims you don't honor is hypocritical and does more harm than good. You must walk the walk and talk the talk.

Now and then I hear of executives who say, "Since we need a mission statement, let's put one together by copying the best from what we can collect from other companies." This is not a good way to form a mission statement. It has to come from the heart and soul of a company. If not, people will see it for what it is–a sham. While a mission statement appears easy to compose, in truth, it requires deep thought because it must define who your company is in a highly condensed statement.

18

THE BIG PICTURE

Do not say to yourself, "My power and the might of my own hand has gotten me this wealth." But remember the LORD your God, for it is he who gives you power to get wealth, so that he may confirm his covenant that he swore to your ancestors, as he is doing today.

—Deuteronomy 8:17–18

Business annals are filled with stories of talented entrepreneurs who started a business with big ambitions but failed because they lost focus of the big picture. To anyone embarking on a new career, I say, "Keep your eye on the doughnut, not the hole in the doughnut."

It's so easy to be distracted, particularly in a small start-up company because, as the owner, your job description will have you acting as everything from your firm's shipping clerk to its top salesperson. Running a one-man show requires spending time tending to miniscule chores and many distractions grab your attention. But what other option is there when an important letter must be sent to a major customer? If you're the only one to write it, that letter becomes your top priority. While a single letter is an easy task, the real headache is the endless drudge-work always needing to be done. The sum total of these routine tasks can seem overwhelming.

Although the typical entrepreneurial enterprise is initially a one-person show, to grow a business, you must delegate responsibilities to others. Attempting to do everything yourself can make you lose sight of the big picture–great organizations are the result of many people's talents working together as a unit.

To outsiders, other people's success looks easy. But it rarely is. It takes years of hard work and sacrifice to succeed. Success is the eventual manifestation of all those seeds planted when companies are in their infancy–new business owners working out of their homes and their spouses getting involved in support-staff chores (such as my wife did). During this period of struggle, demands will be made on you to perform many arduous tasks. You'll discipline yourself to do them because you understand this is the price you must pay to reach your destination. It's a long journey, and along the way, you will acquire considerable knowledge and develop many skills. It is a journey that will make you grow strong.

So many things requiring absolute focus when starting a company, assuring it will be challenging. In my case, I was consumed with attracting the right talent to our organization; concurrently, I worked incessantly to build strong relationships and develop partnerships to firmly establish our customer base. Erecting a solid infrastructure and securing direly needed financing were always foremost on my mind. These vital components demanded an inordinate amount of my time. At the same time, I had to perform those countless routine details that must be done in every business. Looking back, I see that a slight lack of focus could have resulted in my losing sight of the big picture and consequently derailing what was then a fragile enterprise. To stay on track, I constantly referred to a favorite verse of mine in Hosea 4:6: "My people are destroyed for lack of knowledge." In this context, knowledge is synonymous with vision. How well I understood that I must focus on our vision and inspire others to follow our example.

Around here, I'm referred to as the eternal optimist, always seeing a silver lining. Some people call it pollyannaism, but I'm convinced a positive attitude is essential in building any business. If you dwell on the negative, counterproductive thoughts distract you. Negative thoughts are emotionally draining; they sap your energy. Focus on making your vision a reality rather than worrying about all the reasons why it won't happen. You don't want to be like a deer that looks into the headlights of an oncoming car and freezes in its tracks. Nor can you be like an ostrich that buries its head in the sand. The tightrope you must walk requires a delicate balancing act. You must be optimistic with a dash of realism. With this balance, you can maintain an awareness of potential problems, while responding positively to an agenda that demands your full attention.

Many biblical heroes succeeded thanks to their ability to block out distractions. Imagine, for instance, the singular focus required by Noah to build his ark, especially during a severe drought. In spite of ridicule from his neighbors, he stayed on task. He was committed to completing the ark. Later in the Bible, Job underwent terrible trials without cursing or denouncing God. He took comfort in his belief that the Almighty would provide for him.

Genesis 26 tells the story of Isaac, who became very wealthy, possessing vast holdings of fields with large flocks and herds in the land of Beersheba. When his enemy, the Philistines, filled his wells with earth, Isaac dug more wells, which were again and again ruined by the Philistines. However, Isaac never lost faith. Instead, he focused on digging more wells. Observing his faith in God and persistence to keep building wells, King Abimelech of the Philistines was impressed with Isaac's faith. Abimelech realized that Isaac had a covenant with God and agreed to stop destroying his wells. Like Noah and Job, Isaac saw his determination and faith sanctified by God's blessings.

The small businessperson is not the only one who might miss the big picture–large companies and entire industries can have myopia, too. In fact, in a classic article titled "Marketing Myopia" that appeared in *Harvard Business Review* in 1960, author Ted Levitt described how the buggy whip industry became obsolete at the turn of the twentieth century after the introduction of the automobile. Levitt claimed the buggy whip's demise resulted from industry leaders failing to realize they were in the transportation business. Manufacturers felt threatened by the new contraption they referred to as the headless horse; instead of switching gears to make automobiles, they retrenched. Shortly thereafter, the demand for buggy whips evaporated.

Likewise, the motion picture industry almost did a deep six when television made its debut in the early 1950s. Here, too, was a failure to see the big picture. Movie moguls, instead of thinking of themselves as being in the ever-expanding entertainment business, limited themselves to being in the motion picture business. Nearly a decade had passed before they finally realized their products weren't limited to movie theater screens. To their good fortune, they realized that their production studios were also capable of producing programs for television.

In the 1970s and early 1980s, IBM was Wall Street's darling, consistently ranked as the nation's most admired company. Big

Blue was so successful in its dominance of the mainframe segment of the computer industry that the company failed to acknowledge the coming of the personal computer. As a consequence, tiny start-up Apple Computer got a running head start over IBM, one of the world's most biggest and most profitable companies. IBM's other big faux pas was its failure to recognize the potential of the software segment of the computer industry, a segment with more potential than the hardware side. Bill Gates saw an open window that Big Blue had overlooked, and today, his company, Microsoft, has larger market capitalization than IBM.

My former employer, Federal Express, also recognized a window of opportunity when it entered the overnight delivery business–by doing so, it filled a void in the marketplace simply by delivering mail faster than the post office. Had the U.S. Postal Service been effectively doing its job, Federal Express might have never been formed. This was another case of myopia–postal authorities couldn't think outside the box; they failed to see the big picture.

It's interesting that my first jobs in corporate America were at Union Pacific and, later, Federal Express. Both of these companies were in the transportation business–Union Pacific transported freight and passengers, and Federal Express transported packages and letters. And today, I view my company, WWT, as a transporter of information. I see the big picture and I don't limit the scope of our company to computer technology.

Today at World Wide Technology, we're looking ten, fifteen, or twenty years into the future. We believe the systems we're developing are reshaping the supply chain, and the processes and corresponding technology we're working on will greatly impact the future of the Internet. In this role as a trendsetter, we will determine how people do business in the future.

As God alerted the Israelites in Deuteronomy 8:17–18: "Do not say to yourself, 'My power and the might of my own hand has gotten me this wealth.' But remember the LORD your God, for it is he who gives you power to get wealth, so that he may confirm his covenant that he swore to your ancestors, as he is doing today." As I have prospered with God's help, I am always mindful that what he has given me is for the benefit of others. While we may be beneficiaries of God's blessings, he blesses us knowing we will take what he gives us and pass it on to others. The blessings World Wide Technology receives will be passed to our future employees and their families as well as our customers, vendors, and the community. We are caretakers of what we have today but it is not ours–it belongs to future generations. As the Scriptures tell us, we are responsible for two generations. That's the really big picture.

19

DEALING WITH ADVERSITY

My brothers and sisters, whenever you face trials of any kind, consider it nothing but joy, because you know that the testing of your faith produces endurance; and let endurance have its full effect, so that you may be mature and complete, lacking in nothing.

—James 1:2–4

During my adolescence, few things came easy for me. I struggled in high school, barely eking out a C average. As a freshman I tried out for football, but at five-foot-seven and only 125 pounds, I didn't make the team. I had the height for basketball but was too skinny and didn't make the team until my junior year. Plus, I had such a bad speech impediment and stutter that I took special elocution classes. And because I had an extreme case of shyness, I had little confidence in myself. About the only thing I had going for me was my perseverance. I probably just didn't know any better, but once my mind was made up, I had the tenacity of a pit bull.

During my senior year, my basketball coach said, "You're a decent player for high school, Dave, but don't even think about playing in college. You're so thin, those big college guys will eat you for lunch."

So what did I do? In the autumn of 1969 I enrolled at Central

Missouri State, a school with a student body of thirteen thousand, and went out for basketball. A Division II school, its schedule included nationally ranked non-conference Division I schools such as Illinois State and Texas Tech, so if I made the varsity, I'd be playing with the really big boys. During my college years, I had grown to my present height of six-foot-five–definitely the tallest person in my family's history. When anyone asks my mother how I got so tall, she says, "David wanted to play basketball so badly, he *willed* himself to grow tall." I was still as skinny as a rail, and even though I didn't make the team during my freshman year, I attended every team practice. Evidently the coaching staff was impressed with my grit and determination because as a sophomore, not only did I make the team, but I was given an athletic scholarship. By my senior year I had put on some weight, and with my stick-to-it-iveness I had actually become a fairly decent college player.

Playing at Central Missouri was a great experience. The team flew to some of our away games, so for the first time ever, I was on an airplane. And it was with the team that I sat down to my first meal in a restaurant.

The same tenacity I applied to basketball prepared me to enter the workforce after my graduation in November 1973. I earned a B.S. degree in business administration with an emphasis in industrial organization. However, with only average grades and being African-American, companies didn't come knocking at my door with job offers. A few weeks later, I got a substitute teaching job with the public schools in St. Louis. I enjoyed working with kids, but working part-time made it difficult to make ends meet. I kept applying for other jobs, and five months later I was finally hired by the Boy Scouts of America. I had been in scouting, starting as a Cub Scout and finishing as a Life Scout. The troop in my hometown, Troop 435, was a whites-only troop, and to this day, I remember how my mother and I both cried because they wouldn't accept me. Consequently, some of my friends and I, along with our parents, formed Troop 225, the first integrated troop in Clinton. I credit my scouting experience for helping me get the Boy Scouts job. Still, because I was working for peanuts, I kept on sending out résumés.

A few months later I landed my first job in the business world with Wagner Electric. I started as a supervisor in manufacturing, but about a year later I got laid off. So again, more résumés were mailed out. All in all, starting from the time I graduated college, I sent out about four hundred résumés and averaged two or three interviews a week for three years. After going through a series of interviews with the Missouri Pacific Railroad Company, in February 1976, a dream job came my way: I was offered and accepted a marketing and sales position. The company was committed to hiring African-Americans, and I was one of the first to come aboard. They put me through an extensive fifty-nine-week training program, teaching me all about the railroad industry. I will always be grateful to the company for giving me that wonderful opportunity and investing a year in my training.

Looking back, I consider myself blessed to have had adversity during my youth. A message in Romans 5:3–5 encourages us to stand up to adversity: "Knowing that suffering produces endurance, and endurance produces character, and character produces hope, and hope does not disappoint us, because God's love has been poured into our hearts through the Holy Spirit that has been given to us."

Although I didn't know it at the time, the adversity I encountered as a stuttering thin-as-a-rail kid toughened me up. It developed my character so I could stick with the program when I didn't make the freshman basketball team in college. Making the team as a sophomore strengthened my faith. That prepared me for the two years of hard times bounding around job-hunting before being hired by the railroad. As a consequence, at a relatively young age, I learned firsthand what happens when God removes his hand and allows us to go through adversity so that we may grow stronger. Thelma and I met in 1975, so she was by my side during that period of constant rejection. In retrospect, it was a positive experience for her too, because her faith also grew stronger. And we grew stronger as a team. As the saying goes, "You can't appreciate the sunshine without the rain."

Although I was not aware of it at the time, God was preparing me for the more difficult times I would face as a business owner. In this respect, a person who was protected from adversity during adolescence is in for a rude awakening when the time comes to deal with life's hardships. And believe me, if we live long enough, we'll all have our share of hard times.

The adversities I encountered during my youth served as my training ground for hard times I eventually faced as a struggling entrepreneur. In fact, they were just child's play compared to being strapped with a $3.5 million debt as the owner of a start-up company and with a wife and two young children to support. Believe me, it's not a pretty situation when bankers try to shut you down, monitoring your every move with your suppliers. Nor did I take pleasure when creditors badgered me and called me a deadbeat. Overly aggressive bill collectors made house calls to pound on our door. And then there was the humiliation I suffered when my car was repossessed from the company parking lot one afternoon in 1992.

People often ask, "With so many financial pressures, how were you able to stay focused on your work?" Fretting about my unpaid bills and rising debt would only have compounded my problems. Instead, I knew God was with me, and with my faith in him, I concentrated on what I had to do in order to fix my financial woes.

I persevered through these hard times with a belief that what we were doing for our employees and customers was meaningful. I had faith that our company was capable of providing exceptional value–this enabled me to keep a positive attitude in spite of negative things going on all around me. Yes, I could have easily thrown in the towel and copped a plea that the mountain was too big for me to climb. Instead I pushed forward always focusing on how to someday make a significant difference in the lives of my employees, customers, and vendors. Thelma and I wouldn't allow ourselves to get down. It's always darkest before the dawn, we reminded each other.

Due to the hard times the company was experiencing, it was understandable that employees would jump ship–some did. After all, seeing the owner's car repossessed isn't what you'd call a confidence builder. What would motivate someone like Jim Kavanaugh to stick around, especially since he was privy to our dire financial predicament? When the bank dispatched a full-time representative to our offices to help run our business, Jim was one of the few employees who knew the man was actually a turnaround specialist. Our "in-house banker" was there to protect the bank's interests and look for ways to squeeze money out of us to reduce our debt. During what was undoubtedly our darkest hour, Jim received a job offer that would increase his annual salary over 25 percent. Still, he stayed. Jim didn't leave because he and I shared a vision of what this company would be. We also shared a mutual trust in each other, and because he explicitly trusted me, Jim was willing to invest his time and effort to help put our business back on track. Knowing Jim stood by my side reinforced the message to employees and vendors that there was no need to panic–the company would survive.

People sometimes ask me how much a factor racial prejudice was in shutting doors in my face. Sure I had my share of unfair treatment, as have all African-Americans at some time or another. However I never dwell on it because doing so would be self-defeating. Everyone–no matter what skin color–should recognize that some people will throw stones at you. They don't want you to be successful, but you must refuse to let them distract you. Even when others are looking for ways to pull you down, your job is to focus on Christ and his purpose for you. As it is written in Deuteronomy 30:6–9, if you love God with all your heart and all your soul, he will take care of your enemies, so you don't have to worry about them. With this scripture in mind, I never saw myself as a victim. Such thinking is self-defeating and therefore hurts me, not my transgressors. And in Romans 12:19, we are told: "Beloved, never avenge yourselves, but leave room for the wrath of God; for it is written, 'Vengeance is mine. I will repay, says the LORD.' " Knowing this, it would be foolish for me to seek vengeance on those who wish to harm me. I'll leave that in the hands of the Lord.

Winston Churchill delivered a commencement speech on October 9, 1941, to the boys at his old private school that is memorable due, in part, to its brevity. The great British prime minister approached the podium, faced his youthful audience, and said: "Never give in–never, never, never, never, in nothing great or small, large or petty, never give in except to convictions of honour and good sense. Never yield to force; never yield to the apparently overwhelming might of the enemy." With that, he walked off the platform without another word. I doubt that anyone in the audience ever forgot his message. Churchill could have spoken for an hour and not have had such an impact.

Giving up was unthinkable to me. Even during those difficult times when my business was hanging on by a thread, I kept focused on my mission to serve others, believing that our employees, vendors, and customers would someday benefit. As we are told in 2 Corinthians 1:3–4: "Blessed be the God and the Father of our Lord Jesus Christ, the Father of mercies and the God of all consolation, who consoles us in all our affliction, so that we may be able to console those who are in any affliction with the consolation with which we ourselves are consoled by God." Here, we are taught to do good deeds for others, even though we ourselves are enduring difficult times. For in doing so, we will not be consumed with our own sorrows, but instead will grow strong by doing well for others. This is God's will, and it is my mission, both in periods of prosperity and adversity.

20

CREATIVITY AND INNOVATION

Now to him who by the power at work within us is able to accomplish abundantly far more than all we can ask or imagine.

—Ephesians 3:20

Each of us has received so much, yet we use only a small percent of what we are given. God has blessed each of us with a miraculous gift: a fertile mind. Created in his image, we are endowed with the capacity to create and innovate. To me this means that with determination, we have unlimited potential to achieve.

Each of us has been blessed with enormous creative capacity that far exceeds that of all other living things on this earth. This gift is not limited only to people in the arts, such as artists, writers, and actors–we have all been blessed. True, those in the arts have a platform on which to express their creativity, and their work often places them in the limelight where they are viewed as creative people. But recognized or not, people in all walks of life can be just as creative, whether their vocation is accounting, engineering, or teaching.

Unfortunately, many people don't have the confidence to express their creativity, and consequently, they rarely use it. This inability is a result of being conditioned to think within specific boundaries. It starts when parents teach children they should not believe in the unseen, and some schoolteachers reinforce this belief. "Seeing is believing," we are repeatedly told. In the classroom, students may be graded based on only one correct answer for each question; a student with a different answer may receive a bad mark. There are no options for another answer. It is not open for debate. However, a different answer isn't necessarily an incorrect answer. For example, even the experts may have different opinions about evolution or interpretations of a Shakespearean play. And depending on the history book, the treatment of Native Americans or a Civil War issue is not uniformly accepted throughout the land. So why shouldn't a student be allowed–and even encouraged–to have a different opinion, and be praised, not criticized for his or her independent thinking. When a young person is repeatedly chastised for expressing a conflicting view, over time he or she may be ostracized. Adults who carry this baggage into the workplace have been programmed by the herd mentality. Consequently they repress their creativity for fear of receiving that bad mark.

To this day, I can remember questioning one of my eighth grade teachers about Christopher Columbus discovering America. This never made much sense to me since there were people living in the Americas long before Columbus got here. "So how could he have been its discoverer?" I questioned. My teacher didn't appreciate my thinking. This same teacher also told my class, "It is a proven fact that the lighter your skin is, the smarter you are." Even being the only African-American person in the class, I wasn't the only student who knew this was untrue. After all, there were different shades of skin color among the white kids, too—and the lightest-colored weren't necessarily the best students.

Many times, managers in the workplace stifle creativity by fostering an environment where new ideas are not welcome, thereby discouraging people from contributing their ideas. These managers are so critical of suggestions that their employees rarely express themselves. "What good is it?" They frown. "Management will either take credit for my idea or will say it won't work."

People are encouraged to express their creativity when they know management respects them. It's a matter of letting people know you care about them. Because when they know you harbor good feelings toward them, they feel freer to express their opinions and ideas. We're reminded of this in 1 Corinthians 13:4–7, which tells us that love is patient and kind, and love is not envious, boastful, arrogant, or rude. Love does not insist on its own way; nor is it irritable or resentful. And love does not rejoice in wrongdoing, but rejoices in the truth. Love bears all things, believes all things, hopes all things, and endures all things. While Paul attributes these endearing qualities to love, I believe they are also appropriate in supervising people. Paul's advice teaches us to use patience and nurturing in order to allow people to grow more comfortable expressing their ideas. When we put our staff before ourselves, we help them achieve their goals, inspiring them to contribute their creativity to the organization. In my mind, putting our personal goals and egos aside and focusing on their needs is a way of expressing love in the workplace, and people respond to that in a very positive way.

At our company, people are encouraged to express their ideas and seek better ways to serve others. I may have been blessed to have a vision on the direction in which I believe this company should go, but I also make it known that new and better ideas are always welcome. An open environment where people feel comfortable expressing their ideas means that at any time, someone may come up with a new and better way to do things. Some of our best ideas come from unlikely sources within our organization. By encouraging people to take risks–and giving them freedom to make mistakes along the way–people understand they will be rewarded for good suggestions and not punished for an idea that doesn't work out.

Creativity and innovation are not synonymous. Creativity is thinking up new things and innovation is doing new things. As someone once said, ideas are a dime a dozen, but the men and women who implement them are priceless. With this in mind, a good idea can be suggested over and over, but without implementation, it's of no value. Of course, creativity must be encouraged so fresh ideas are put on the table. But the next step requires that an idea with merit be nurtured; otherwise, nothing happens. Remember it's the execution of the idea that benefits the company. Nothing is accomplished when a lot of ideas generate discussion and memorandums, but then die on the vine. So while I value creative ideas, I also treasure people who have the talent, commitment, enthusiasm, and persistence to see them to completion.

While creativity and innovation are not synonymous, they certainly complement each other. This is aptly articulated in Isaiah 41:6–7: "Each one helps the other, saying to one another, 'Take courage!' The artisan encourages the goldsmith, and the one who smooths with the hammer encourages the one who strikes the anvil, saying of the soldering, 'It is good'; and they fasten it with nails so that it cannot be moved." Here we are reminded that we must work together, praising and encouraging each other, so that the sum total of our efforts becomes greater than our individual efforts.

An organization's most valuable asset is not its people, but the right people in the right position. Good management gets the most out of its assets. Tragically, some managers unwittingly waste the potential of this rich resource, while other managers, capitalizing on their people's creativity and innovation, prosper.

21

FIRE IN THE BELLY

I know your works; you are neither cold nor hot. I wish that you were either cold or hot. So, because you are lukewarm, and neither cold nor hot, I am about to spit you out of my mouth.

—Revelation 3:15–16

A friend of mine who manages a stock brokerage office told me about an interesting interview he had with a job candidate. "I was talking to a twenty-two-year-old man just out of college who had a major in finance," my friend said. "Something he said to me really got my attention.

" 'Some of my friends wanted to be ballplayers or doctors when they grew up,' the applicant said. 'But all my life I've wanted to be a stockbroker.' "

My friend explained his policy of hiring only college graduates with a minimum of five years' work experience. The applicant responded, "If you give me the opportunity to work here, I'll be the best stockbroker you ever hired. I only ask that you give me a chance to prove myself, and you can mark it down in your date book: 'Today I hired the best stockbroker I ever hired.' Mark my words, I will be this office's number-one salesperson."

My friend's gut feeling prompted him to go out on a limb. "I believe you. Congratulations. You've got yourself a job." And you know what? He's that company's number-one producer today.

Halfway through my friend's story, I knew how it would end. Why? Because I would have hired the young man too. That's because he had fire in the belly. Only a person who really planned to be top salesperson could make such a statement believably. When I hire someone, I look for that fire in the belly–not just what is said but how it's said. There is a definite correlation between attitude and altitude. It's a person's attitude that determines the altitude–how high he or she will go.

In Revelation 3:15–16, Jesus describes his thoughts on people's attitudes: "I know your works; you are neither cold nor hot. I wish that you were either cold or hot. So, because you are lukewarm, and neither cold nor hot, I am about to spit you out of my mouth." I also have an aversion to lukewarm people. I'm interested in people who are enthusiastic and want to make a difference in other people's lives. I'll hire a person with a positive attitude every time over a more qualified person who's negative. We can train the positive person but we don't even want the negative person around our people because as the saying goes, one bad apple can spoil the whole barrel.

It's a two-way street: Enthusiastic people with a burning desire to serve others are generally attracted to an atmosphere where other dynamic, positive people work. When I started my company, I didn't have much to offer but a positive, can-do attitude. What we have today, we didn't have back then, things such as an attractive work environment and competitive compensation with a strong benefits package. We did, however, have passion, and, one employee at a time, good people came aboard–individuals with fire in the belly who wanted to make a difference in people's lives. They were attracted to our organization because they could feel our excitement and energy. We made up for our lack of tangible enticements with passion and energy–the foundation of our organization. Today it is an integral part of our culture.

When a company's management cares about people and does right by them, the best job candidates are attracted to it. As the saying goes, Birds of a feather flock together. Many businesspeople are driven mainly by profit, and they are willing to compromise their principles for money. Employers who shortchange their customers by offering inferior products and services will use similar tactics with their employees. In the long run, good companies attract and retain good people.

Once again, all of this radiates outward to vendors and customers. When guests visit our premises, they sense this attitude. It surfaces with the warm reception at the front desk; it's reinforced by wholehearted smiles and friendly greetings from our employees. All guests have to do is walk through our facilities and see our people are at their workstations. They can sense the excitement. It's easy to see our people feel good about themselves, secure in the knowledge they work for a caring company. Visitors feel the mood; that's because it's the real deal. It can't be faked. Our atmosphere generates good feelings. We've all experienced this feeling–if not in the workforce, in other environments when we visit homes of loving families, classrooms of dedicated teachers, and houses of worship where communicants live their lives by the teachings of their god. In a like manner, I believe this feeling of benevolence should be fostered in corporate America.

Sports analogies provide good examples of how fire in the

belly works, because results are measured on the game's scoreboard. For instance, we've all seen a football team come from behind to win the game. In sports, they call momentum "the big mo," but what causes it? Often, it's one fired-up player whose determination and desire inspires teammates to put forth a herculean effort. Similarly, in basketball, a team rallies because a particular player takes the lead with a "hot hand." That leadership sparks the entire team until the whole team is on fire too. Off the field, momentum works in the business arena, and here too, like a sports team leader, a company leader's enthusiasm spreads throughout the organization. When excited employees pass it along to vendors and customers, sales soar.

With the knowledge that God is by my side, coming to work every day to serve others is a driving force that inspires me. Here, I can fulfill my purpose that God has given me. As it is written in 2 Chronicles 31:21: "And every work that he undertook in the service of the house of God, and in accordance with the law and the commandments, to seek his God, he did with all his heart; and he prospered." Great achievements happen when you have a passion that comes from the heart.

22

MENTORING

The good person out of the good treasure of the heart produces good, and the evil person out of the evil treasure produces evil; for it is out of the abundance of the heart that the mouth speaks.

—Luke 6:45

The Doing Business by the Book classes were the catalyst for writing this book. Here, on Sunday mornings, Thelma and I mentored thirty-five or so people, teaching them how to prosper according to the Scriptures. My business, along with these classes, serves as our ministry to touch the lives of many people.

Although we present a weekly lesson to each class, everyone is invited to participate. Class members tell personal experiences, explaining how their faith in the Word of God has contributed to their success. These testimonies of success encourage class members to keep pushing forward despite challenging times. The purpose of this exercise is to reinforce their faith, to confirm they are following the right path, and reaffirm their source. The listener thinks, If it happened to them, it can happen to me. As the Scriptures say, the Lord has given each of us a measure of faith. What he did for them, he will do for you.

Every fifth Sunday, our class is conducted in a conference

room at the Faith House, an organization devoted to helping abandoned children. These Sundays give me the opportunity to talk to the children. At a recent class, I asked a twelve-year-old boy what he wanted to do when he grew up.

"I want to play in the NBA," he said.

"Have you ever considered being a businessman?" I replied. "Maybe then, you can someday own a professional team. Imagine what it would be like to be the owner of an NBA or NFL team? The owner can hire and trade the players. Besides, a player's career only lasts a few years. You can own the team all your life–and you can sell it at a profit or pass it down to your children to own someday."

He smiled and looked interested. The thought had never occurred to him. I want all young athletes to know who runs this country. Certainly, there are professional athletes who are excellent role models for our children–but many aren't. Besides, I like to inspire young boys and girls to think about business careers, not just the more glamorous careers in the limelight such as professional sports and show business. One reason is that the odds are so overwhelmingly against making it in those professions that it's not a realistic ambition for the vast majority of youngsters. Then, too, the impact a businessperson can have on society is potentially much greater, especially when you consider what he can do to better the lives of employees and customers. Consider too that a business can live far beyond the life of its founder. An average NFL career only lasts about four years, and afterward a young athlete, still in his mid-twenties, must find another productive way to spend the rest of his life.

Being a mentor to young people is a responsibility I enjoy.

It's a way I can pay back the mentors I had as a young boy. Among them were my parents, scout leaders, and coaches. All my life, I have been blessed in receiving so much support from so many.

Early on in my career, my mentor was George Craig, a marketing vice president for Missouri Pacific Railroad Company. I was one of the first African-American sales and marketing people hired to represent the company, and there was considerable concern about sending me around to make sales calls. Now you have to remember that back in the seventies the treatment of African-Americans was much different than today, particularly in markets such as southern Louisiana and southern Texas, my sales territory. Mr. Craig made sure no one within the company tried to interfere. By the time I formed my own company, Mr. Craig had retired, but he continued to support me when I began offering auditing services to railroad companies. He was well respected in the railroad industry and opened many doors for me. All he had to do was give me his stamp of approval. "David Steward is okay," he'd say to one of his cronies. "He's someone you can trust. Here's an individual you can do business with." Mr. Craig gave me access to people with whom he had long-term relationships, which provided me with instant rapport.

Another important mentor of mine was Luke Fouke, a real-estate developer ten years my senior. We met back in the eighties when I rented my first office building from him. Luke, a Yale graduate, comes from a prominent, old-line St. Louis family. His social background and private schooling helped him develop lifelong relationships that happen to include many of the city's most influential businesspeople. He demonstrated his confidence in me again and again by introducing me to his contacts. Although he gained nothing personally from it, he did it to help me. I've since had the pleasure of mentoring Luke's son, giving him some advice on business. That was just a small token compared to what Luke did for me, but I suspect Luke's biggest reward is the delight he has in seeing me succeed.

I am forever grateful to all the people who helped me along the way, for how well I know that nobody can do it alone. Knowing this, I am committed to helping others; giving to them makes me feel I am the one that is truly blessed.

Whenever I'm asked how to find a mentor, I always answer, "Seek out a successful business owner who will give you spiritual guidance."

I offer this advice knowing everyone needs someone to take them to the Word of God, guide them scripturally, pray with them, and lift them up when they need inspiration. A person with a business has experienced ups and downs. Finding such a person is not difficult because many people use biblical scriptures as foundation principles to conduct business. These individuals have a sense of morals, ethics, and loyalty–they're committed to making a difference in other people's lives. They're not driven by the desire for money but by the desire to serve others. I suggest finding a mentor who has good character–something that cuts across religious affiliation. For instance, I've had some wonderful Jewish leaders who have advised me, lifted me up, and supported me in my efforts to help others.

When you mentor, it's a win-win situation because both parties receive. As Jesus tells us this in Luke 6:45: "The good person out of the good treasure of the heart produces good, and the evil person out of the evil treasure produces evil; for it is out of the abundance of the heart that the mouth speaks." Here we are taught that giving is ingrained in our hearts and, when we mentor, it is our heart that reaches out to help others.

23

A COMPANY IS KNOWN BY THE PEOPLE IT KEEPS

Whoever walks with the wise becomes wise, but the companion of fools suffers harm.

—Proverbs 13:20

The business adage, "People are a company's greatest asset," should be modified to read: "The *right* people are a company's greatest asset." Generally there is no shortage of people, but finding the right people for your company can be a real challenge.

Each year, many Fortune 500 companies recruit on the campuses of the business schools at leading universities across the country. I can't quarrel with hiring college graduates at the top of their class, but I believe there are even more important criteria than high intelligence or advanced training. At World Wide Technology, we seek out people with the right attitude. It's crucial to put the best talent into the right slot within the organization. But equally important, those individuals must have good character. That's why we emphasize qualities such as integrity, loyalty, and trust. We seek people who are giving and want to make a difference in this world.

Jesus tells a parable in Luke 6:43–45 that provides an excellent lesson on hiring the right people. He says that a good tree will not bear bad fruit, nor will a bad tree bear good fruit. Hence a tree is known by its own fruit. Jesus explains that figs are not gathered from thorns, nor are grapes picked from a bramble bush. Likewise, a person with a good heart does good deeds; an evil person will do evil deeds. In this parable, Jesus expounds that you can separate the two by listening carefully when people speak. To do this, you must listen not only to what is said, but you must hear what comes from within. This is true because what comes from the heart reveals character and attitude. As the Scriptures tell us, from the abundance of the heart, the mouth speaks.

An often-overlooked hiring criterion is selecting those most likely to adapt to your corporate culture. Simply put, those who aren't a good fit will likely leave on their own accord, or stay on as poor team players negatively affecting morale. Avoiding either scenario requires extra time and effort in your hiring process. That's what it takes–many hours carefully screening recruits and asking the real questions. Plus, you must carefully listen and scrutinize everything you observe, including eye contact, facial expressions, body language, and tone of voice. This tedious job pays off in the long run in terms of reduced turnover and increased productivity. Keep your radar out for job candidates who share your company's values.

For instance, a restaurant owner I know looks for people who enjoy serving others. Right off the bat he tells them the job requires working evenings, weekends, and holidays, his busiest times. He explains up front, "You're gonna be here New Year's Eve, Mother's Day, and the Fourth of July when everyone else is having fun with their families." Then he asks for their comments and carefully observes their reactions. "If I detect an unwillingness to work during these times, they're not for my restaurant. Past experience tells me a certain type of person who derives great satisfaction from serving people in the food business is the guy I'm on the lookout for."

Checking employment records and references is essential. Look for strong recommendations by former employers and coworkers. Pay close attention to past achievements in entirely different arenas. For instance, a standout college athlete is likely to be disciplined and a good team player. The Bible tells us we will know them by their fruits. Oftentimes, people's reputations precede them. For instance, a job candidate who plays an active role in the community is probably a giving person. Coming from a good family also speaks volumes for an individual's character. As they say, the apple doesn't fall far from the tree. Those who work with professional recruiters rely on recruiters' reputations knowing they won't send poor candidates because they value their relationship with you. A headhunting firm performs a valuable prescreening service by evaluating job candidates before dispatching them to your office.

A definite spiritual atmosphere prevails at World Wide Technology. Everyone here knows I live and manage by the Word of God, and there is an undercurrent of Christian counsel and ministry. Though we don't conduct prayer meetings and certainly don't discriminate against nonbelievers, an atheist might not have a strong desire to work here. While being a Christian is not a prerequisite for working here, some of what we believe is likely to rub off on anyone who's with us every day. In 1 Corinthians 3:1–2, Paul, one of Jesus' disciples, refers to people who were not spiritual as infants of Christ. Thus, he fed them with milk rather than solid food. Here, Paul tells us that a full-course dinner is of no use to a baby. Babies need milk for their nourishment; likewise, we feed small doses of the Word of God to our people and minister them in this way. Today, people of many faiths work at World Wide Technology, including Hindus, Jews, and Muslims. The lessons of the Scriptures strike a true chord with all people.

Let us also remember that a diverse workforce constitutes strength. As America draws strength from being a melting pot with a diversity of people from many nations, a company also gathers strength when it employs people from many cultures because this assures a cross section of thinking. It's like an exquisite quilt with patches of different fabrics, colors, shapes, and sizes, each adding to its overall beauty. A diversified organization has many perspectives from which to draw and find solutions.

Good leaders surround themselves with good people. They know that to thrive, they must attract the smartest people available–including employees who are smarter than they are. Conversely, weak managers are prone to shy away from employing smart people due to their personal insecurities. They fear their jobs may be jeopardized if their people outshine them. Not so! To excel, any organization must continually seek the best available people. As Proverbs 13:20 says: "Whoever walks with the wise becomes wise, but the companion of fools suffers harm." A good leader must not only surround himself with smart people, he willingly gives them sufficient authority so they can make decisions and act in what they think are the best interests of the company. If you are continually reining your people in, your company cannot advance. The level of confidence and trust you give is what you get back.

Many World Wide Technology employees hold a position at

a supervisor's level or better. I place a lot of weight on their willingness to promote a subordinate or make a recommendation for advancement in another department of the organization. Someone who does this has his or her heart in the right place–this giving individual wants to help others. As it says in Proverbs 3:27: "Do not withhold good from those to whom it is due, when it is in your power to do it."

24

BRANDING

Either make the tree good, and its fruit good, or make the tree bad, and its fruit bad; for the tree is known by its fruit.

—Matthew 12:33

While name brands play an important role in today's commerce, branding actually dates back to the Stone Age, around 5000 B.C. Proprietary markings appeared on pottery from around this time, and in southwestern Europe, cave drawings depict bison with symbols on their flanks, markings presumed to identify ownership. Archeological diggings have unearthed fired clay pots from around 3200 B.C. identifying their makers.

During the Roman Empire, between 500 B.C. and A.D. 500, early documents suggest trademarks were commonplace. Latin literature refers to "maker's marks" on an array of items including cheese, wine, lamps, medicine, ointment, metallic ornaments, and glass vessels. These were the first products identified to enable early shoppers to make a buying decision based on the reputation of the maker. Much like today, a craftsman's reputation was a good predictor of the quality of merchandise. Throughout Europe, merchants working within guilds were not permitted to advertise; consequently, quality assurance was provided by trademarks that identified a product's maker. Later, between the fourteenth and seventeenth centuries, a "merchant's mark" was evidence that a merchant traded in goods acquired from reliable sources. Then, as now, an establishment's reputation was judged by the brand-name products it sold. During the same period, trademarks were popularized by armorers, metalworkers, papermakers, tapestry weavers, smiths, tanners, goldsmiths, and silversmiths.

In modern times, a brand name represents that goods bearing its mark will be uniform in quality because they are manufactured or controlled by the same company. With reputable brands, there is significant goodwill associated with the reputation of an enterprise. With so many product choices and with two-family incomes resulting in reduced discretionary time, Americans have never been more dependent on the assurances provided by brand names. Consequently, consumers are shopping at fewer stores and buying more brand products. A brand is synonymous with a company's reputation. This is true not just for consumer products; brands determine where we do our banking, invest our money, and receive our health care. With life insurance policies and retirement plans, we prefer to put our trust in institutions with reliable reputations so we can have peace of mind: We feel assured they will honor their end of the bargain in the distant future.

In a parable found in Matthew 12:33, Jesus offers advice on how to choose a vendor: "Either make the tree good, and its fruit good, or make the tree bad, and its fruit bad; for the tree is known by its fruit." An individual's reputation as well as a company's lets people know what to expect. This is as true today as it was in biblical times.

As the world shrinks and international multibillion-dollar companies conduct business around the globe, their brands become their most valuable assets. In the case of Coca-Cola, reputed to be the world's most recognized product, its brand name is undoubtedly its most valuable asset. Founded in 1886 when pharmacist John Stith Pemerton first concocted a syrup-like formula to heal his patients of ailments ranging from the common cold to sore throats, today Coca-Cola is sold in more than two hundred countries and has a market capitalization of about $135 billion. Analysts concur that this market value is based on the company's brand, more so than the total of all of its tangible assets. Its formula was never patented; had it been, it would have become public domain decades ago. While, back in the early 1900s, figuring out the exact formula would have been a formidable task, today's sophisticated laboratories have the capacity to break it down, analyze it, and come up with soft drinks to challenge the "real thing." Without "Coca-Cola" on the bottle, however, it is unlikely that another company's beverage could sway loyal Coca-Cola customers to switch to another soft drink.

Of course, brand loyalty such as Coca-Cola and other companies enjoy must be earned. Consumers flock to brand names like IBM, Merrill Lynch, and Southwest Airlines for good reasons. These companies established reputations by consistently providing exceptional products and services. Such reputations don't happen overnight; they are earned one customer at a time.

And as great institutions establish brands, individuals can too. For instance, brand-name actors are paid millions of dollars because they are proven box-office attractions. Today, Bill Cosby is one of the world's most highly paid entertainers. He also receives huge fees for product endorsements. But Cosby was by no means an overnight success. It took many years of hard work, consistency, and perseverance to establish his show business career. Today Cosby is a brand name, and accordingly, attracts millions of fans willing to buy tickets to see him perform. And because his good name stands for quality, consumers are persuaded to buy products endorsed by him.

An original oil painting may sell for a million-plus, again based on an artist's reputation. A renowned artist may not possess more talent than an unknown but able artist–yet his or her signature on the canvas can add a thousand times more value to its price tag. Likewise, consumers choose to buy books written by best-selling authors, and in this respect, an individual writer's brand name attracts large numbers of readers.

In addition to famous entertainers, artists, and writers who command large salaries, many people have established themselves as brand names in the business arena. Included in this elite group are individuals such as Oprah Winfrey, Donna Karan, Ralph Lauren, and Tiger Woods.

You don't have to be a movie star, television personality, or business mogul to be a brand name in your profession. A restaurant owner, dry cleaner, or dentist–anyone who does exceptional work and establishes an outstanding reputation in his local community–can be considered a bankable brand for his specialty. Likewise, you can work for a company and distinguish yourself as a leading expert within your own area–top salesperson, buyer, researcher, technician, and so on. Once you earn such a reputation, your employer will recognize your value, and other companies may even try to lure you away. Be the best in your field–known for your integrity and commitment–and the world will beat a path to your door.

You may be the reason why a certain account does business with your employer. Customer loyalty is often based on a single individual. In this respect, you are the brand name that wins customer loyalty for your entire company.

At World Wide Technology, we try to differentiate ourselves with superior work in everything we do. At times we may spend money on a project above and beyond what's necessary. But we do it because we know, in the long run, our reputation is our most valuable asset, and that's the price we pay to keep our reputation intact. Our investment helps assure our brand name is hailed as best in its field. Over time, it pays off because customers and suppliers tell others about our extra effort. This word-of-mouth attracts business as well as people who want to work for us. Indeed, your reputation–your brand–is your most valuable asset. It's something nobody can take away from you; only you can take it away from yourself. You must keep earning your reputation every day.

A good reputation built over a lifetime can be lost overnight. In Luke 16:10, Jesus says, "Whoever is faithful in a very little is faithful also in much; and whoever is dishonest in a very little is dishonest also in much." In building your brand, quality and the best service you can provide can never be compromised, not on your smallest job, not for your most unassuming customer. To do so would jeopardize your reputation with your customers and your employees. You must consistently do your best–always.

25

BEING A TECHNOLOGY-DRIVEN COMPANY

My people are destroyed for a lack of knowledge.

—Hosea 4:6

Unquestionably, the Internet is the biggest thing in commerce since the invention of the printing press. Millions of people who go online every day have difficulty recalling life without it. There may be a time in the future when not having knowledge of how to get online will be analogous to being illiterate.

Today, U.S. companies are spending hundreds of billions of dollars to build their e-business infrastructure to communicate internally with employees and externally with customers and business partners. It's far more than a matter of convenience; it's a matter of survival. To compete in today's marketplace, a company must incorporate state-of-the-art Internet technology to furnish its employees and customers with necessary and timely information. The Internet enhances an organization's visibility and, most importantly, it provides value to customers by reducing overhead, and, in turn, decreasing price points. Note too that it provides ways to give more value to customers at no additional cost to them.

We live in exciting times. What's currently happening with the Internet dwarfs the Industrial Revolution. Think about it. Today, the efficiency with which we can move information–anytime, anywhere, and to anyone in the world–has opened vast opportunities that boggle the mind. As it is written in Hosea 4:6: "My people are destroyed for lack of knowledge." How appropriate in today's technology-driven business world. Any organization that resists e-business is destined to go the way of the dinosaur.

In my organization, technology is not only our business, it's what runs our company. We constantly strive to improve supply chains and create efficiencies to provide additional information to our customers; technology connects us to our suppliers. In the future, the biggest winners in all industries will be companies able to design systems that cater to varying vertical markets in defining their supply chains. These companies will capture the greatest market share in their respective industries.

Information Technology (IT) is an extraordinary tool that provides knowledge to everyone–employees, vendors, and customers. Today, information can be transferred via the Internet in microseconds around the world. The existing information available to businesspeople as well as consumers is so vast, it was hardly imaginable just a decade or so ago. As a result of modern technology, dramatic change has occurred in the entire business process. Change occurs so rapidly some people find adjusting to new ways difficult. Having been indoctrinated to think two plus two equals four, they cannot comprehend that so much more is involved today. That's because they've been acclimated to think a certain way, and now find they must adjust to a new standard.

To compete in today's environment, all companies must be

technology-driven so they may realize certain efficiencies. This requires large investments. Again, as the Bible says, sow seed back into your business, which necessitates building infrastructure. Remember, if you don't sow any seed, how can you reap a harvest? Still, some companies using old methodologies have been successful in their industries and have made substantial bottom-line profits. You might say their previous successes have become their own worst enemy, because they have become rigid and resist change. Thus they are not going forward, and smaller, more nimble, entrepreneurial companies adaptable to change are taking advantage of this window of opportunity. In time, the bigger but slower-moving companies are destined to lose their competitive edge.

The advances in technology we witness today are only the tip of the iceberg. Technological changes are occurring exponentially. Companies that fall behind may lose so much ground that it will be difficult for them to catch up. To adapt to and implement necessary technology demands the full support of an organization. This means the entire company culture must embrace change–that's every aspect of a company–marketing, sales, operations, accounting, finance, everything. To gain a competitive edge, a company must focus on technology. While investment in technology is costly, it's minuscule compared to the cost of standing still. As the Red Queen advises Alice in *Through the Looking Glass*, "Now, *here*, you see, it takes all the running *you* can do, to keep in the same place. If you want to get somewhere else, you must run at least twice as fast as that." Author Lewis Carroll could have been referring to today's rapid changes in technology. Those who resist changes in technology will eventually become obsolete. Staying in the same place is indeed comparable to going backward.

Today, for companies wanting to stay ahead of the curve, state-of-the-art IT is essential to serve your internal people. It allows employees to communicate with one another and enhances their ability to acquire knowledge. Externally, IT opens many avenues to serve suppliers and customers. By integrating your systems with suppliers and customers, strong partnerships can be built. Here too, relationships are established based on well-grounded foundations via strong communications.

Today's Internet may be foreshadowed by a parable in John 6 that tells about a large crowd near the Sea of Galilee that followed Jesus and his disciples up a mountain. Upon seeing many people coming toward him, Jesus said to Philip, "Where are we to buy bread for these people to eat?" Jesus was testing Philip because he knew what he was going to do. Philip replied, "Six months' wages would not buy enough bread for each of them to get a little." Andrew, one of his disciples, said, "There is a boy here who has five barley loaves and two fish. But what are they among so many people?" Jesus instructed his disciples to have the crowd of about five thousand families sit down in a grassy area, and so they did. Then Jesus took the loaves and gave thanks to his Father. Afterward, he distributed the loaves to the people and everyone was given as much fish as they wanted. Afterward, Jesus told his disciples to gather up the fragments left over so nothing would be wasted. The disciples obeyed his request and the fragments of the five barley loaves left by those who had eaten was enough to fill twelve baskets. After witnessing what had happened, those who were present said, "This is indeed the prophet who is come into the world."

Similar to Jesus' feeding of the multitudes, with technology we are able to feed information to the multitudes that would not otherwise be available. This technology is so great, it allows fragments that are left over to be utilized elsewhere. Our obligation and responsibility is to use this technology to serve others and to feed his people. Through technology, we can provide access to knowledge that can make an enormous difference in the lives of multitudes all over the world.

26

ACCENT THE POSITIVE

If you do not doubt in your heart, but believe that what you say will come to pass, it will be done for you. So I tell you, whatever you ask for in prayer, believe that you have received it, and it will be yours.

—Mark 11:23–24

When I started my business in 1990, not many people thought an African-American from a small rural town like Clinton, Missouri, could come to St. Louis and build a billion-dollar technology company. But what they didn't know was the vision I had about starting my own business. Nor did they know how much faith I had that we would succeed.

I refused to let anyone's negative remarks distract me. The odds were already stacked against me, and had I believed what they said, there'd be no need to even get out of bed. I would have been defeated before my feet hit the floor.

What I did have going for me was my faith in God. I *knew* what was possible according to scripture. The Bible is indeed the most incredible book on positive thinking ever written. As it says in Romans 8:28, "We know that all things work together for good for those who love God who are called according to his purpose."

Now that's what I call a positive statement: Believe in God and conduct yourself based on his teachings, and good things will happen in your life. To my way of thinking, this says it all. According to the Word, all things are possible.

Jesus was a strong advocate of positive thinking. He allowed himself to be crucified, even knowing his holy purpose for being here on earth. He willingly gave his life, mindful his death would serve generation after generation after generation. God sacrificed his son for our benefit. Seeing that Jesus acted positively on our behalf, I refuse to allow myself to entertain negative thoughts. Knowing that God is on my side reassures me. My faith grants me an abundance of strength, and I am always observant that failure is not an option. I *know* we will succeed.

As a CEO, I must lead people with positive thoughts. Over the years, I've been asked questions such as, "How's your company doing in this terrible economy?" and "With the demise of so many Internet companies, how are you faring?" My stock answer is, "Great!" Even when we were in the start-up stages and $3.5 million in debt, I said, "Great!" Why? Because I believed it. Today, my friends and fellow church members say, "We never realized you went through difficult times." They never knew because I always maintained a positive attitude–the joy of the Lord is my strength. I knew we'd get through the tough times and that something much better was going to come. My people and I were enthusiastic, excited, and full of fire. We never allowed ourselves to be consumed with doubt. We knew we would succeed. The glass was always half-full, never half-empty.

Nothing drags you down faster than constantly second-guessing yourself; being consumed by doubt is self-defeating. As Jesus told his disciples in a parable in Matthew 17:20, if your faith is only the size of a mustard seed, you can move mountains, so nothing is impossible for those who believe. What an inspiring message. We can achieve anything that we can conceive. If we have faith, we can move mountains.

Speaking about the impossible, I have always been inspired by Abraham's unbending faith in God. He was one hundred years old and his wife, Sarah, was ninety, according to Genesis 17, when God made a seemingly implausible covenant with Abraham that his wife would bear him a child. Yet, the following year, Isaac was born. Through Isaac and future generations, Abraham became the father of many nations. As Abraham never lost faith in God's promise that Sarah would be the mother of his son, I also have an unshakable faith that God will always be by my side. With his guidance, I know it is not possible to fail. As a constant reinforcement, I read Psalms that fill me with reassurance and confidence and give me a clear focus on God. I enjoy Psalms 91, 103, and 104, and I recommend them for spiritual uplifting.

The Bible teaches us not only to love, but it repeatedly tells us to be forgiving. In a wonderful lesson on forgiveness in John 8:4–11, the scribes and the Pharisees brought an adulteress to Jesus. They said to him, "Teacher, this woman was caught in the very act of adultery. Now in the law Moses commanded us to stone such women. Now what do you say?" They were testing Jesus, trying to entrap him to speak out against the law. Jesus promptly replied, "Let anyone among you who is without sin be the first to throw a stone at her." There was a silence and one by one, beginning with the elders, they went away. When Jesus was alone with the woman, he said to her, "Woman, where are they? Has no one condemned you?" She said,

"No one, sir." And Jesus said, "Neither do I condemn you. Go your way, and from now on do not sin again."

In Matthew 18:21–23, again Jesus teaches us to forgive. In this parable, Peter asks Jesus, "Lord, if another member of the church sins against me, how often should I forgive? As many as seven times?" Jesus answered, "Not seven times, but, I tell you, seventy-seven times." Throughout the Scriptures, we are told to love and forgive, forgive and love. What positive thoughts. Being bitter, spiteful, and unforgiving are negative thoughts. These are thoughts that harbor resentment. When you have brooding thoughts about someone, you tend to dwell on them, but what good comes from that? Chances are, the subject of your resentment isn't even aware of your feelings. As a consequence, you're the only one who suffers, because negative thoughts distract your focus from your real mission. Hence, your valuable time and energy are wasted seeking retaliation when it can be more wisely spent concentrating on achieving God's will for your life.

As Jesus taught his disciples in Mark 11:23–24: "If you do not doubt in your heart, but believe that what you say will come to pass, it will be done for you. So I tell you, whatever you ask for in prayer, believe that you have received it, and it will be yours." These positive words are words of power that I live by.

27

COMMUNICATING WITH PEOPLE

What I say to you in the dark, tell in the light; what you hear whispered, proclaim from the housetops.

—Matthew 10:27

A common denominator shared by many successful leaders is strong communication skills. I'm not talking about dazzling an audience with a dynamic speech. Sure, being an excellent orator is a major plus. But equally important is staying in constant touch with people in many little ways, keeping them current on what's going on with the company, both internally and externally. At WWT, we routinely communicate with our people via memos, phone calls, newsletters, e-mails, bulletin boards, small group meetings, town hall meetings, and so on. In short, we take advantage of all available forms of communication to stay in touch.

As CEO, I'm constantly making sure our people understand our vision, the company's mission, and our short-term and long-term goals. I don't want anyone to feel left in the dark. I want everyone to know what we stand for, so he can share our beliefs and know he's a valued team member. I constantly remind our people they represent our company–to each other, to our customers and vendors, to the entire community.

Our executive team is routinely addressing small and large audiences within the company–always telling them the bad news along with the good. Sure, there are times we could just post messages in the company newsletter or e-mail our key managers and ask them to pass it on to others, but when something's really important, we want everyone to hear it directly from us. Every quarter, we make a special address to all employees, reviewing our progress in meeting our annual goals in the past three months. In addition to talking about the good things going on, I give them the brutal facts–financial information, the challenges we face–everything. They not only hear about company wins, we're up front with them about our losses and objectives we failed to make. They deserve to be well informed about everything going on in the organization because they have as much stake in this company as anyone, including myself. So we don't pull any punches. When there's bad news to report, everyone is told. As members of our team, they're privy to all the vital information, just as I am. Here, I am following the advice Jesus gave in Matthew 10:27: "What I say to you in the dark, tell in the light; what you hear whispered, proclaim from the housetops."

Keeping others in the dark is a sure way to hurt morale. First, they'll hear all kinds of rumors through the grapevine–some accurate, others far-fetched. Second, closing them out is a sure way to build barriers within the organization, and that's demoralizing. When you keep your people informed about your problems, some among your troops may surprise you with solutions. Past experience has taught me that solutions can sometimes come from unlikely sources.

Just as you communicate both the good and the bad to your people, they should feel comfortable coming to you with problems. But if you're one of those bosses who shoots the messenger, your people aren't likely to volunteer what they know. So instead of jumping all over the bearer of bad news, express your gratitude that a matter was brought to your attention, whether or not it was music to your ears. In the movie *The Godfather*, Tom Hagen, the consigliere played by actor Robert Duvall, has a wonderful line. When a Hollywood director flatly refuses to do business with "the family," the consigliere informs him, "I must go to the airport. The Godfather wants to hear bad news immediately." Yes, even an organization like the Mafia realizes a don needs people to come to him with bad news.

We encourage our people to communicate bad news, and while we prefer to hear it in person, they can tell us via the suggestion box, on the phone, by letter, through e-mail, even anonymously–we welcome it all. The important thing is to make others feel comfortable communicating with us. Too often, people postpone bringing a problem to the attention of the boss–and consequently, it goes unnoticed until the damage is already done. Sometimes their discomfort is due to an invisible barrier a boss has put up that keeps bad tidings out. Inadvertently, or sometimes intentionally, an "us-versus-them" relationship exists dividing workers from managers. Managers can symbolically separate themselves from their workers in many ways. Some companies have dividers such as executive dining rooms, executive bathrooms, and plush executive suites far removed from people down the ladder. These barriers can be removed only when executives stop hiding in their ivory towers and come down to meet with people at their workstations.

In his book *In Search of Excellence* Tom Peters refers to "Management By Walking Around" (MBWA). He recommends managers walk the floor and talk to their workers to find out firsthand what's happening in the workplace. I'm constantly walking the floor, meeting with people, chatting with them, making small talk—always keeping in mind that if they don't feel comfortable with me, how will I know what they're *really* thinking? In order for MBWA to be effective, I make the rounds by myself. I walk the floor and meet with managers, shipping clerks, secretaries, everyone—on a one-to-one basis. I've seen some CEOs make rounds surrounded by an entourage of executives. Consequently, their contact with employees remains impersonal and intimidating. It rarely happens that a worker will stand up before a group of executives to express his true feelings or voice disapproval.

To make people feel comfortable, I do not sit behind my desk when someone visits my office. The desk is a barrier, so I walk around it, and sit in a chair beside them or across a small coffee table. Even better, when I want to meet with someone, I'll visit him in his office, where he feels most comfortable. This way, I can talk to him about the photos of his family on his credenza or the award displayed on the wall. Sure, my reason for the visit may be business-related, but I also make it a little personal. This way, I show my interest in him as a person—he's more than just a cog in a wheel to me.

I remember reading that some American politicians who visited Vietnam during the war met only with generals and other top brass. When they got home, they reported the fighting from what they were told in the comfort of officers' headquarters, not on the battlefield with the troops. As a result, they were privy only to statistical information and not what was going on in the trenches, where they might have found out firsthand what was really happening. The same thing is true of getting the right information from vendors and customers. You have to leave the comfort of your executive headquarters and meet them on their turf. This is so important, I spend about 50 percent of my time on the road, calling on customers and vendors, quizzing them about how I can better serve them. Most importantly, I'm letting them know I care about them–communicating loud and clear that they're my highest priority.

Nobody can express gratitude for a customer's business quite like the CEO or owner of a company. While I would like to do this with every customer, time constraints don't permit me to see everyone. But I do it with our biggest customers. Nothing compares to a CEO or business owner who shows a customer that his business is appreciated. It's as if the entire company were saying, "Thank you." When the owner of a small clothing store waits on you and says, "This is the outfit that looks best on you–it's what I personally recommend," it makes your day!

There is much reference in the New Testament to Jesus' excellent communication skills. For instance, Luke 2:47 describes a time when, as a boy, Jesus spoke in the temple in the presence of several rabbis. They were amazed that a young person could have so much understanding and be so articulate. Matthew 7:28 describes people reacting to Jesus' speaking ability after he delivered a lengthy sermon. Here too, the crowds of people were astounded at his teaching. It is written that they were impressed at how he spoke with authority, yet he was not a scribe.

A wonderful storyteller, Jesus liked to use parables. In a time when few people were able to read or write, easy-to-remember parables were an effective way to keep a listener's attention. Note that the great speakers of our time were proficient storytellers. Two of our greatest orators come to mind: Ronald Reagan, known as "The Great Communicator," and Martin Luther King, Jr., America's great civil rights leader. Both knew how to win their audiences by sprinkling their speeches with anecdotes.

The Word of God cuts across time, and through the parables and other teachings Jesus presented to his disciples, he continues to speak to us today. I communicate his words to my people every day. Since people are at different stages in their lives and with their acceptance of the Word of God, I am constantly assessing people and feeding them what I think they can digest. I am aware that some people are not as far along as others, and accordingly, I meet them where they are. And I am always respectful to people whose religious beliefs differ from mine.

While I have a mission to spread the Word of God, specific beliefs are not a prerequisite for hiring or advancement at WWT. Certainly there are many good people in other denominations, and there are people with integrity and a strong work ethic who are not involved in organized religion. I enjoy working and communicating with the variety of people we have at WWT.

28

NOTHING HAPPENS UNTIL SOMETHING IS SOLD

I have fought the good fight. I have finished the race. I have kept the faith.

—2 Timothy 4:7

The job of selling does not rest solely on the shoulders of salespeople calling on customers. The entire staff is the sales team. At our company, every employee's job description includes a link to the sales effort, so, in effect, everyone sells. Everyone at WWT is aware that without sales, the company would cease to exist. So, for good reason, our company reveres our salespeople; you might even say we give them hero status.

I got my start in sales, and I have always been proud to be a salesperson. I've paid my dues. I spent years out there pounding the pavement, making call after call, and like all salespeople, I had my share of down times, spending long days away from my family without getting an order. Yes, it can be discouraging, especially when your paycheck is commission-based. What always kept me going was my belief in what I sold, my knowledge that the customer would receive a good value. Any salesperson worth his salt understands there are days you can't even give your product away, let alone sell it. It's all part of the business. Many people believe selling is a numbers game: If you make enough calls, you'll make sales. I've always admired salespeople who have grit and determination, who believe in their product and their company, and who refuse to give in no matter how much resistance they face.

Michael Jordan once talked about the numbers in his basketball career, which I think is a good analogy to a sales career. "I've missed more than nine thousand shots in my career," he said. "I've lost almost three hundred games. Twenty-six times I've been trusted to take the winning shot and missed. I've failed over and over again in my life. And that is why I succeed." Good salespeople think this way. They put up with broken appointments, doors slammed in their face, and impolite customers. They believe in their mission and refuse to let rejection defeat them. How well they understand the words in 2 Timothy 4:7, which could have been written just for them: "I have fought the good fight, I have finished the race, I have kept the faith."

I like the adage "The sale doesn't begin until the customer says no." This is true because if the customer starts out ready to buy your product, you haven't really sold anything. With this in mind, an actual sale results from convincing a prospect who doesn't think he needs your product or service that he does. Many novice salespeople accept a "no" as a final answer and immediately stop selling. They quit because they fear they'll encounter sales resistance and be accused of high-pressure selling. A thin line exists between high-pressure selling and persistency. Oftentimes, you just have to keep selling even though the customer has expressed a lack of interest.

With experience, a seasoned salesperson can determine when to continue and when to walk away. But when you stop too soon, you could do a disservice to your customer–who truly needs your product.

As CEO, most of my time is spent selling. About 50 percent of the time, I'm in the field meeting with customers and vendors. Most of the rest of my time involves meetings with our own people, and I have to sell them, too. Believe me, it's essential that I have their support–if they can't be sold, the project gets canned! I never take it for granted that they're automatically aboard. Often, it's necessary to field their questions, and if there's resistance, we discuss their objections and schedule additional meetings for more discussion. No matter how much I believe in something and want it to move forward, a project that lacks support is doomed to fail. So if I can't sell them, there's a good reason–and it's likely to be some detail I overlooked.

Before I can sell anything–a product, service, idea, whatever–I have to believe in it 100 percent. That's why I say, "The sale starts by selling yourself." If you haven't bought into it, you're in for a tough time convincing someone else to buy into it. For the record, I have never tried to sell anything to anyone that I wasn't sold on. Your conviction is a vital part of the selling process. This is true because your belief in your product comes through loud and clear. When you believe in it, your words exude passion. Your enthusiasm becomes contagious and affects your prospect's point of view. Most importantly, your conviction signals your sincerity as well as your integrity.

Conversely, when a salesperson doesn't believe in what he sells, he may not realize it, but a negative message is sent. Prospects subconsciously pick up signals from body language, facial expression, and tone of voice, and consequently, doubt consumes them: They become hesitant and unable to make a buying decision. Here's how it works: A while ago, Thelma and I went shopping on a Saturday afternoon to buy her a new car. We knew the model we wanted, the price we were willing to pay, and we were looking forward to driving her new car home. The salesman, however, hemmed and hawed during the sale, and we began to feel hesitant and unsure about buying the car. I started to think that we should probably shop around at other dealerships. We left the showroom, disappointed because we didn't accomplish our mission, which was to buy a car. Not only did that salesman waste our time, he let us down. Had the salesman had conviction and confidence that it was right car for us, I'm sure the outcome would have been a sale. My experience was a case of a salesperson's hesitation becoming contagious when it should have been his enthusiasm that was contagious!

Our sales team is one of WWT's greatest assets, and as I mentioned, I make a lot more sales calls than a typical CEO. Of course, not all CEOs enjoy selling like I do. Certainly some with backgrounds in finance, engineering, and manufacturing may meet with customers infrequently. While I believe selling is one of my most important responsibilities, it may not be the forte of all CEOs—some of whom excel in other areas and have successful careers. Those who do not actively participate in sales delegate that responsibility to capable people.

Speaking of sales representatives, in Exodus 4, Moses asked God to send someone else to speak on his behalf, explaining that he was not articulate. When Moses persisted in his plea, God told him to seek Aaron, who was a fluent speaker. God told Moses that he would give him instructions on what to say, and then Moses could teach Aaron what to say to the Israelites. So even in biblical days, salespeople were recruited, instructed, motivated, and dispatched to tell their story.

29

THE JOY OF WORK

By contrast, the fruit of the Spirit is love, joy, peace, patience, kindness, generosity, faithfulness, gentleness, and self-control. There is no law against such things.

—Galatians 5:22–23

It's been said that if you enjoy your job, you'll never work another day in your life. Yet to some people, finding joy in work is an oxymoron. Someone once said to me, "You're not supposed to enjoy it. That's why it's called 'work.' " In *Webster's Collegiate Thesaurus*, a synonym for "work" is "drudgery."

It's a pity to have a negative attitude about work. That kind of thinking not only makes work boring and tedious, it causes stress that sometimes leads to health problems. In addition, a negative person in the workplace can hurt the morale of coworkers. The negative effect can extend to customers and vendors. Think about the last time a grumpy waiter served you at an elegant restaurant. Forget the delicious aromas and ornate decor–a surly server can turn what could have been an evening of fine dining into an awful experience. The same applies to a crabby clerk behind the ticket counter at the airport. One person's bad day can cause a domino effect, causing other people to have a bad day.

Conversely, when you have passion for your work and truly

enjoy it, it will come across to people in a delightful way. That's why, in an interview, I place a strong emphasis on a job candidate's attitude. Generating laughs has become such a mainspring in Southwest Airline's culture, job candidates are sometimes asked during an interview, "Have you ever used humor to solve a workplace problem?" By asking the right questions and listening carefully, I'm able to determine who will enjoy the job and work in harmony with our people. Many individuals are referred to us by employees and friends of the company, so for starters, someone believed they'd enjoy working here. We seek people who have a successful track record–men and women who developed a reputation at their previous job for putting passion into their work.

We also want someone who enjoys serving other people. I can't wait to come to work each morning so I can make a difference in the lives of others. I don't work to make money; as the adage goes, money works for you. It's a wonderful feeling to go home at the end of the day knowing you put in a good day's work. Sure, there are days when I'm dog-tired, but no matter how exhausted I might be, I feel so good about having that sense of accomplishment. There's also great satisfaction knowing I impacted other people's lives, realizing I have contributed my part to what God has ordained me to do. When you're part of a team, it's particularly rewarding to know you didn't let others down. This is what I consider a true blessing. I feel sorry for people who just go through the motions at work–constantly looking at the clock, just waiting for quitting time. You can spot them by the way they start straightening their desks half an hour before their shift is over, getting ready to make a beeline to the nearest exit. Those clock-watchers miss out on the joy of work. What a pity!

I remember how excited I was about landing my dream job at Federal Express. I thoroughly enjoyed what I was doing. Then when I was assigned to a new boss, my positive attitude changed. While I still loved my job–and was successful at it–I no longer derived joy from it. It was because I had a boss who didn't like himself, and this was reflected in how he treated people. He received no joy from his job, and as a result, he didn't inspire anyone under him. He also lacked integrity; his word meant nothing. Eventually he was replaced, but his shortcomings taught me a valuable lesson about how the lack of passion for one's work has a demoralizing effect on others. As a consequence, not only did I vow to nurture passion for my work, I became determined to spread it to others.

Like the grumpy waiter at an otherwise enjoyable meal, a grumpy boss can negatively affect everyone around him. Some CEOs are so impressed with their titles and take themselves so seriously that their pomposity and arrogance make people feel uncomfortable in their presence. Consequently, people don't feel free to step outside the box. This stifles creativity and innovation. Such a work atmosphere is destructive, and it destroys the incentive to excel. People working in an environment like this are not inspired to go above and beyond the call of duty. They simply do what's necessary to keep their job. They may put in their time, but their heart is not in their work.

When the doors of my company first opened, I was determined it would be a place where people would have lots of opportunity to grow, have a sense of purpose, and at the same time, have fun. Some people think the workplace isn't the place for fun, but I disagree. In fact, at WWT, we work hard to have fun; it's ingrained in our company culture. Don't think we don't take our work seriously, because we do–we fully believe we provide an important service to our customers, and the well-being of our families depends on how well we do it. To my way of thinking, that's serious business. We just believe that people can be very serious about their work *and* have fun. I think that's a good formula for success for every business.

A case in point is Southwest Airlines, the only airline to continually generate profits year after year for the past twenty-five years. Founder Herb Kelleher always insisted on having fun and is said to have looked for three qualities he considered a must in anyone he would hire: enthusiasm, a great attitude, and a sense of humor. The company encourages the laughter and fun that are at the core of the Southwest culture.

There are many stories about Southwest employees having fun with customers. My favorite is the one about a passenger who nearly missed his flight. While the plane waited for him, a petite flight attendant climbed into the overhead compartment above an unoccupied seat. The other passengers were aware of what was happening and everyone waited with anticipation for the man to board the plane. After he was escorted to the vacant seat, he opened the overhead compartment to place his bag and the flight attendant greeted him: "May I help you with that, sir?" Everyone laughed hysterically, including the surprised man. Nobody seemed to care that the plane departed late.

Surveys show that Southwest employees are considered among the most loyal in the U.S. workforce. No doubt some of their loyalty has to do with how they enjoy themselves at work. And, the people who fly the airline are among the most loyal customers in the airline industry. This shows that having fun can indeed be a way to succeed in business. As it says in Galatians 5:22–23, "By contrast, the fruit of the Spirit is love, joy, peace, patience, kindness, generosity, faithfulness, gentleness, and self-control. There is no law against such things." I believe the fruit of the Spirit should exist everywhere–there is no reason to exclude it from the workplace.

At WWT, I don't hide the fact that I have a sense of humor, and when I put my levity on display, others know it's okay to exhibit theirs, too. I encourage it because humor makes people feel comfortable, which, in turn, enhances their freedom of expression. A joke or cute story is a good icebreaker to relax people before a meeting. It's also a good way to keep people's attention during a lengthy session filled with detailed information. For instance, I recently served on a company committee where a slide presentation was made, and about halfway through a seemingly endless number of slides with graphs and technological data, suddenly my image appeared on the screen–a photo taken in the seventies. There I was for all to see, wearing a great big grin and sporting a huge afro. Everyone laughed hysterically, and no one more than I.

Laughter is a wonderful antidote for dealing with adversity. As we're told in James 1:2–4, we should consider setbacks as joy because they are a test of our faith that produces endurance. Thus, we become stronger. What a great way to face trials and tribulations–look a temporary setback squarely in the eye, laugh at it, and then do something about it.

30

THE ART OF LISTENING

Listen to advice and accept instruction, that you may gain wisdom for the future.

—Proverbs 19:20

Most communication experts agree you should do more listening than speaking. To quote Mark Twain, "If we were supposed to talk more than listen, we would have two mouths and one ear."

It's hard to listen and talk at the same time, and since there's much to be learned by listening, a wise person understands the virtue of letting others speak. In Mark 4:23–24, Jesus advises his disciples: " 'Let anyone with ears to hear listen!' And he said to them, 'Pay attention to what you hear; the measure you give will be the measure you get, and still more will be given you.' " There is more to be learned by listening than by monopolizing a conversation. In addition to receiving input, the astute listener wins friends and influences people. Why? Because respect given to others will be abundantly returned.

Typically, leaders are expected to have good speaking skills. Early in life we learn this premise. As schoolchildren, we see our teacher address us from the head of the class, and throughout college, we are subject to classroom lectures by instructors and professors. The same situation exists with clergymen, judges, committee heads, board chairmen, and so on–leaders speak and others listen. We take it for granted that an effective communicator articulates thoughts intelligently; this does not negate the importance of possessing equally proficient listening skills. In today's world of business, a manager who fails to listen is no better than a mute leader.

A good business leader listens carefully to employees, suppliers, and customers. Concurrently, they are keenly aware of that attentiveness and willingness to listen, which promotes exchange, a free flow of communication between them. By listening, focusing on the message, and being careful not to interrupt, a good leader demonstrates respect for the right of others to express themselves. This expression of faith generates goodwill at all levels of industry. Internally, barriers between management and personnel are removed; likewise, externally, bonds are strengthened with suppliers and vendors.

Good listeners pay attention to what they hear and, when appropriate, ask pertinent questions. Their inquiries underscore their interest and stimulate the other party to volunteer additional information. Pertinent questions also enable leaders to gather additional information. Often, they will be open-ended questions such as: "By this you mean . . ." "How will this affect . . ." or "What is your opinion?" A question of this nature requires more than a yes or no answer–it gets an explicit response.

Astute questions accomplish the fact-checking required to determine the correctness of input received. By listening acutely, you can ascertain what is credible information. At times people will be dishonest; they may have ulterior motives. Nonetheless, a thorough cross-examination enables you to judge right from wrong. Again, you must ask the right questions. You may want to restate the answers to confirm what you heard and then wait quietly for a response.

When the Lord asked King Solomon what he wanted, the king asked for wisdom. Thus, God blessed him with wisdom. Solomon was smart enough to know that with wisdom, he could obtain riches, so he did not request wealth. In Proverbs 19:20, Solomon says: "Listen to advice and accept instruction, that you may gain wisdom for the future." As King Solomon advised, it is wise to listen so you may be well informed. It turned out that Solomon's wisdom made him one of the richest men of his time.

Still and all, being a good listener without corresponding action is unproductive. We've all seen the manager who goes through the motions of listening to employee and customer complaints. "Thank you for bringing this to my attention," the manager says, nodding in agreement. "Your point is valid and I will give it some study." Afterward, while some discussion may occur, nothing really happens. Days and weeks pass and in time you realize the issue is no longer on the agenda. After a while, people acquainted with the manager's lack of follow-through realize it's a waste of time, so they stop voicing their complaints and suggestions.

When our company had only a handful of employees, I was able to personally listen to everyone. And while today I have an open-door policy, welcoming employees to meet personally with me from time to time, my schedule does not permit me to meet with every employee. As I discussed in Chapter 3, "Delegation" (Exodus 18:17–23), Moses was advised by his father-in-law, Jethro, to delegate to able and trustworthy individuals who represented many tribes. Jethro recommended that Moses "set such men over them as officers over thousands, hundreds, fifties and tens. Let them sit as judges for the people at all times; let them bring every important case to you, but decide every minor case themselves. So it will be easier for you, and they will bear the burden with you."

Like Moses, today's business leader must set up a chain of command to avoid being burdened with minor issues that can be resolved by others. On major issues, a good leader will get personally involved. And, as in Moses' day, different contingents within an organization have different agendas. At times, several department heads may offer contradictory ideas to a CEO, but it may not be possible to reach a consensus. Here, a CEO must prudently listen and assimilate a wealth of information. Finally, the man or woman at the top makes a decision. Whether or not it is popular with everyone, hopefully it will be the right decision for the organization.

31

GOOD LEADERSHIP IS LOVE

This is my commandment, that you love one another as I have loved you.

—John 15:12

Not a single business school in the U.S. offers a course in love. And while business school curriculums do list a variety of leadership studies, the subject of love is not discussed. Yet Jesus, the greatest leader ever, advocated that we should love each other. These were not idle words–Jesus commanded it. This was his last command before ascending to heaven.

Rarely is love a topic of discussion in business circles, especially among Fortune 500 companies. Over the years, I attended many leadership seminars, and not once do I recall the subject of love on a program. Admittedly, railroad and overnight freight delivery managers are macho guys; certainly they're not what you'd call warm and cuddly. Just the same, good leadership principles apply to all fields, whether you're managing day-care providers or NFL football players.

The first letter of John in 1 John 4:7–12 tells us to love each other because love comes from God. Those who do not love, do not know God, whose love was revealed to us when he sent his son into this world to be the atoning sacrifice for our sins. Since God loved us so much, we also ought to love one another. And while no one has ever seen God, if we love one another, he lives through us and his love is perfected in us. This scripture lets us know that we are put on this earth to love one another. My love for my fellow man isn't confined to my immediate family. Knowing that God is in me, I have an unlimited supply of love. So great is this supply that I can love everywhere, including the workplace.

I don't try to hide my love at WWT. I love our employees, our vendors, and our customers. I confess I don't go around blurting out to people how much I love them–not that anything's wrong with that. However, many people in today's society aren't ready to hear it said out loud. So instead, I declare my love for them through my actions. I am here to serve them, and they know it. Their needs come first, before mine. This explains why I made sure my employees never missed a paycheck when we had severe cash flow problems, even though I had to skip a few of my own.

I express my love by showing my people respect–for instance, by my willingness to listen to them. I demonstrate how much they mean to me by inviting them to share my vision and my dreams. I provide opportunities for advancement. I display my care for them by making sure our company stands for quality and integrity in every aspect of our business. I value the company's reputation, understanding that each of their reputations is on the line with mine. These actions express my love for our people.

The above are intangibles, but there are also many tangible expressions of love at WWT. We have a wonderful health-care plan for our employees and their families, 90 percent of which is paid for by the company. And since we are concerned about their future after they retire, for the past six years the company has matched—dollar for dollar—the money employees put into their 401(k) plans. Likewise, our compensation plan is set up to reward their contribution to the company's success.

We treat our people as though they are family, and we treat their families like family, too. This was our motivation to extend exceptional health-care benefits to their families. Additionally, throughout the year, we have family-oriented events including barbecues and parties. Our suites for professional baseball, football, and hockey games are always filled with our people and their family members. And we always feed them well at these events. When we treat them to a good time, we do it first-class. That's because we think they deserve the best we can give them.

A good leader demonstrates his love for his people through his fairness in his decision making. This is illustrated in one of my favorite biblical stories, 1 Kings 3:17–27. This scripture gives an accounting of how King Solomon judiciously handled a delicate situation when two women went to him to solve a dispute. The two women lived in the same house and both had claimed giving birth to a son. One infant died at childbirth; and now each mother claimed the surviving child was hers. After King Solomon heard each woman insist that she was the rightful mother, he called to a servant to bring his sword to him. He then said, "Divide the living boy in two; then give half to one, and half to the other." Immediately, one of the women cried out, "Please, my lord, give her the living boy, do not kill him." The other said, "It shall be neither mine or yours; divide it." With this demonstration, the king said, "Give the baby to the first woman. She is the mother."

Like King Solomon, there are times when a good leader must

select one individual over another to promote. In such cases, diplomacy prevents bitterness. This is akin to a parent who is in the awkward circumstance of having to favor one child over another: a mother must decide which child will receive a one-of-a-kind family heirloom; a father of two has only one extra ticket for a football game, and so on. In all such cases, a good leader, or a good parent, must act so that everyone's dignity is preserved.

In Galatians 5:6, it is written, "The only thing that counts is faith working through love." How true. Faith is based on love. My people know I put them first. From where I stand, their best interests come before everything else, including my own. They know I am there for them and I do everything I possibly can for their benefit. Serving them is my number-one priority. I commit myself to keep their careers intact, safe, and secure. When you do this for people, they respond by being loyal, caring employees. Who says love doesn't belong in the workplace? I know it does. I've been blessed by being able to express love to my people–in many ways–and it is being returned to me in kind.

32

THINK BIG

Have faith in God. Truly I tell you, if you say to this mountain, "Be taken up and thrown into the sea," and if you do not doubt in your heart, but believe that what you say will come to pass, it will be done for you. So I tell you, whatever you ask for in prayer, believe that you have received it, and it will be yours.

—Mark 11:22–24

Growing up in Clinton, Missouri, a small town 230 miles west of St. Louis, I lived on the wrong side of the tracks–literally. Being only a stone's throw from the railroad tracks, the small frame home on our family's six-acre plot of land was in a perpetual state of vibration. My parents raised my seven siblings and me in a house next door to my maternal grandparents', a house that we have since torn down so we could build a new home for my mother, where she lives today. I owe my strong work ethic to my father, who was a mechanic, a part-time janitor, and a trash collector. He also moonlighted as a night watchman and a server at holiday parties for the town's more affluent families.

We were poor, but I personally never felt like we were. That's because my parents always put food on the table for us, and there was always a roof over our heads. Some of what we ate came from the few cattle and hogs that my siblings and I were responsible for. Every morning before school, my farming chores included milking the family cow and making sure the hogs were slopped. I attended Franklin Elementary School, on the other side of the tracks, where I was the only African-American boy in my class.

How we lived was quite a contrast to the lifestyle of the white kids. Even so, my mother kept telling us that we should never resent anyone who had more than we had. Again and again, she said, "You can do anything you set your heart to, son, and someday you'll have all those nice things too."

My mother always took us to church and made sure we attended our Sunday school classes. Our small church was too poor to have its own minister so it had one that came once a month to conduct our Sunday services. Our lay leaders held services on all other Sundays. The adult members used to say to me, "Little David, play on your harp." I felt blessed to be referred to as David, the shepherd boy, because he was one of my favorite biblical heroes.

The members of our church believed in the Lord, and we had hope and faith that God was going to deliver us. Even as a young boy, I knew all things were possible through Christ Jesus, who strengthens us. So instead of being limited by my depressing circumstances, I looked beyond the confines of my small hometown and focused on my vision of what God had in store for me. As a young boy, I knew someday I'd live in St. Louis, even though most people in our neck of the woods felt intimidated by "the big city." The few young people who left town migrated to nearby Kansas City or Springfield, small cities in comparison to St. Louis. To make it in St. Louis was big-time–like the lyrics in the song "New York, New York." In my case, I knew if I could make it in St.

Louis, I could make it anywhere. During my teens, I frequently visited my older brother Phil in St. Louis, so, at an early age, I decided that was where I'd someday live.

When I was a youth, one of my favorite scriptures was the story about Shadrach, Meshach, and Abednego in the Book of Daniel. These three Jews lived in a province of Babylon under the rule of King Nebuchadnezzar. The king built a golden statue standing sixty cubits tall and six cubits wide and decreed that everyone must bow and worship this statue. Those who failed to obey his mandate would be thrown into a furnace of blazing fire. Shadrach, Meshach, and Abednego refused to bow down to the statue, declaring that they would not worship a false god. Their defiance enraged the king, who ordered them bound by the strongest guards of the army. The heat of the furnace was raised sevenfold its normal temperature and the three men were thrown into the blazing ovens. The intense heat killed the guards who lifted Shadrach, Meshach, and Abednego into the fire.

While witnessing what appeared to be a certain death sentence, King Nebuchadnezzar saw four men walking in the fire; one had the appearance of God. When Shadrach, Meshach, and Abednego exited the furnace, the king, his prefects, governors, and counselors saw that they had no signs of having been in the scorching oven. Not a hair on their heads had been singed. This prompted King Nebuchadnezzar to declare that the God of Shadrach, Meshach, and Abednego sent his angel to save his servants who trusted in him. The king decreed that any people, nation, or language that blasphemes the God of Shadrach, Meshach, and Abednego would be torn limb from limb. The king then promoted the three men to serve in high positions in the province of Babylon.

This story illustrates that all things are possible with a strong belief and faith in God. Whenever I face adversity, I think of the unbending faith of Shadrach, Meshach, and Abednego, and I realize my own problems are inconsequential by comparison. For instance, at one time, my company was unable to obtain financing from a standard bank. In order to make a deal, we had to pay 22 percent interest on our loans—a rate that makes it difficult to profit. Nobody would have blamed us for pulling in our reins and choosing not to grow our company. But I had a vision to build a big business, and I wasn't about to give up on my dreams. Take Shadrach, Meshach, and Abednego. Had they bowed to a gold statue, they could have been spared the excruciatingly painful punishment that appeared certain. When I thought about the test of faith those three men endured, high interest rates seemed trivial by comparison.

Most often, a start-up company has limited financial resources, so a small business owner must be innovative to survive and expand. In a way, this is an advantage, because it forces one to be resourceful and creative. A small business owner must be nimble and able to turn quickly. This requires creativity, and when partnering with larger companies, a small company must differentiate itself from the competition. When a small company is able to stand out from the pack, big companies notice.

As a small company grows, it goes through four different stages. First, there is the start-up stage, followed by the entrepreneurial stage; next is the growth stage, and lastly, the mature stage. Each stage requires a different set of talents; to expand a business, an owner must personally grow and recognize the importance of bringing the right people aboard, those with different and complementary skills. If the owner can't let go and delegate to others, the business will suffocate.

The downfall of large companies attests that deep pockets don't cure all problems. As a small business grows, so must its owner. An entrepreneur can never become complacent and must continually learn new ways to improve business. To survive and thrive, knowledge is a more valuable asset than money. This lesson is emphasized in a story that appears in 1 Kings 3 telling about King Solomon dreaming he spoke to God. In the dream, God asked Solomon what he should give him. The king replied that God had loved his father, David, and that he was thankful to follow in his father's footsteps and sit on his throne. Solomon then asked God to give him the wisdom to discern between good and evil so he could govern the large numbers of people in the land.

God was pleased that Solomon did not ask for riches or for the life of his enemies, but instead asked for understanding to determine what is right. The Lord granted Solomon a wise and discerning mind, as well as both riches and honor for all of his life. God said that no other king shall compare with Solomon. And on the condition that he walk in his ways, and keep his statutes and his commandments, as his father, David, did, Solomon would be granted a long life.

Like Solomon, people today who place the needs of others above their own will also prosper. And, like Solomon, you can ask in prayer and expect results if you truly believe. We are reminded of this in Mark 11:22–24 when Jesus said to his disciples: "Have faith in God. Truly I tell you, if you say to this mountain, 'Be taken up and thrown into the sea,' and if you do not doubt in your heart, but believe that what you say will come to pass, it will be done for you. So I tell you, whatever you ask for in prayer, believe that you have received it, and it will be yours."

Every big achievement starts in the mind of a person who believes his or her dream is possible. But just thinking big doesn't automatically make things happen. You must first have a positive image of yourself and others–and believe in yourself and others. This lesson is told in Numbers 13, which tells about a time when Moses dispatched twelve spies to the land of Canaan to determine the strength of its people. Upon their return, the spies told Moses that the Canaanites were huge people and so large that it made them feel as small as grasshoppers. They were not giants, rather the spies thought of themselves as small. To lead his people into the land of milk and honey, Moses recognized he must inspire them to see themselves worthy of possessing it. Likewise, in today's business world, success starts with the belief that one is worthy of success.

THE PERSONAL TOUCH

Whoever wishes to be great among you must be your servant, and whoever wishes to be first among you must be your slave. Just as the Son of Man came not to be served but to serve, and to give his life a ransom for many.

—Matthew 20:26–28

Every now and then, do you think back to a more genteel time and begin to long for the "good old days"? If you're like me, you miss the personal touch of the small businessperson–in my case, it was Dotson's, a corner store operated by a mother and her son. I can still visualize her standing in the front of the store, and her son stocking groceries on the shelves or serving as butcher, slicing meat behind the counter. They knew you by your name, and they also knew your parents and grandparents. The farmers would display their produce at the market square in the center of town where we'd buy fresh vegetables. In other small communities, perhaps a pharmacist at the drugstore would pinch-hit at the soda fountain, scooping a dish of ice cream on a slow day. The hardware store owner would take ten minutes to search through bins of nuts and bolts for a nickel's worth of merchandise that you couldn't find. The family doctor made house calls. Those were the good old days.

The small mom-and-pop stores have been replaced by giant-size supermarkets. The neighborhood drugstore is no longer owned by the pharmacist; the soda fountain is gone. You'll find the ice cream in a self-service freezer in the back of the supermarket. The small hardware store has all but vanished, having been replaced by the big-box home service center. Most consumer products we buy today are sold at outlets owned by national chain store operators. We haven't the faintest idea about what their owners' names are.

Yet we cannot always assume a big company is devoid of the personal touch. It's not the size of a company or the number of its employees that alienates people, causing them to yearn for the way things were. Corporate employees should not be pegged as insensitive or lacking in desire to serve others. Not every large multinational enterprise is an impersonal monolithic giant, nor are its employees incapable of caring. The character of a caring, giving person remains intact no matter where he or she is employed.

What does happen, however, is that often people working for a large company don't do many of the things that were done when the company was small. Here, I refer to some of the little personal touches that contributed to the company's early success. For instance, the owner of a small restaurant personally greets all of her customers and knows many of them by name. When her business expands and she operates other restaurants at various locations, she can no longer welcome customers as they walk through the door. (She can be in only one place at a time.) When the owner of a small grocery store expands his business, he stops working behind the counter. His customers miss him because he isn't there to give them his personal attention. The new meat man, for instance, doesn't throw an extra slice of meat on the scale after it's been weighed. Nor does he put aside a prime cut of meat for a special customer like the old butcher did.

Granted, it isn't always possible to give the same personal attention to every customer or employee when you operate a large organization. But there are a lot of little things you and your employees can do to provide that added personal touch to still let people know you care about them. Bear in mind that just as you worked hard to become successful and grow your company big, you must now work just as hard at doing what you did when your company was small. Why? Because it was those little personal touches that got you to where you are today. And when your people emulate what you do, it becomes ingrained in the company culture.

For instance, as the owner of a start-up company, I personally greeted everyone who walked through the front door. When the business grew, I was no longer the person who welcomed everyone; today, the receptionist at the main entrance is the official greeter. I think a friendly receptionist plays an important role in our success, because their warm, courteous welcome is often a guest's first impression of us. In effect, the receptionist represents me, as well as every employee–a warm greeting suggests to each guest that WWT people are friendly and courteous. This is also true when a secretary answers her boss's phone. If the secretary is abrupt and cold, the negative message gets sent that the boss is unfriendly, too. On the other hand, if the secretary is warm and polite, the caller has a positive impression of the boss. It makes sense, doesn't it, because no warm, courteous boss would tolerate a personal secretary mistreating anyone–but a cold, discourteous boss wouldn't bat an eye. A secretary who is condescending to a caller reflects badly on the boss as well. Chances are he's aloof. As Proverbs 16:18 says: "Pride goes before destruction, and a haughty spirit before a fall." Pride is not a strength, but a weakness. It is a sure sign that the ego has inflated one's self-importance. The haughtiness and arrogance that make people feel uncomfortable diametrically oppose the warm feelings fostered by the personal touch.

People at the top of a large organization set the stage for the way people further down conduct themselves. A CEO's courteous, warm personality permeates an organization. Likewise, so will a mean-spirited CEO's personality. For better or for worse, the CEO sets the mood of the company.

I live my life by Jesus' words in John 15:12 commanding us to love one another. I know this scripture applies to every aspect of my business career. Now treating people with love–that's personal. I care for our people, suppliers, and customers, and by placing their needs above my own, I lead by example. And there are many at WWT who follow my example.

Some people think a billion-dollar-plus organization can't treat people like a small company. Does a company's size preclude the ability to reach out to people personally? I say no. Big organizations can have caring individuals capable of adding personal touches to business relationships, just like small companies can. How do I know this is true? Because I do it every day. For instance, I personally sign cards to every WWT employee for special occasions such as birthdays and Christmas. I literally make hundreds of calls in early January to wish people well for the new year. Baby gifts are also sent to employees' newborns. I send get-well cards to our employees and include some of my favorite healing scriptures. Similar cards and Bible passages are sent when a family member passes on. When people are facing adversity such as a sickness or a death in the family, I let them know they are in my prayers. When people are facing business challenges, I invite them to come to our Bible study class. Again, you don't have to be a small business owner to welcome love into your workplace. You've heard me say that leadership is love, and there are many ways to express love in a large corporate environment.

When a customer or supplier visits our headquarters and we have an opportunity to meet, the next day I send a card thanking the individual for taking time to stop by. This is an old habit I practiced when I started my career as a salesman–I always sent a personal note to a new customer to express my gratitude for his or her business. When I come across a newspaper or magazine article about someone I know–whether it's about a promotion at work or an honor received for community service–I mail it to the individual with a brief congratulatory note. I send personal Christmas and New Year's cards to suppliers and customers, usually adding a personal note expressing my appreciation of their services or business. "We were a great team during the past year, and I look forward to a repeat performance," I might say, or "I appreciate your business, and most of all, I value your friendship." Another thing: I constantly send e-mail messages, especially to executives. I know they prefer e-mail correspondence because they're often too busy to read a lot of mail–it's easier and more economical for them to respond via the Internet. I realize that each small gesture by itself may seem insignificant, but strong, long-term relationships are built by doing a hundred little things rather than doing one great big thing once in a blue moon.

I heard that George H. W. Bush used to jot a note to himself on the back of a business card he was handed—the president did this to remember something personal about the person. It was a nice touch, and it's no wonder anyone who had the opportunity to meet the president walked away impressed by his warmth. People close to President Bush loved many little things about him, but the American public wasn't privy to all the little personal touches that inspired loyalty within his inner circle.

Since the beginning of our company, I have shared my dreams, as well as my vision of the company's future, with our employees. Now, sharing one's dreams is very personal. Some business leaders are secretive about such matters—possibly they fear their revelations could become a source of embarrassment if they fail to reach their goals. I think differently. I want my people to share the faith and belief I have in my future, because it's their future, too.

In 2 Corinthians 6:16, God is quoted as saying: "I will live in them and walk among them, and I will be their God, and they shall be my people." Likewise, any CEO can spend some time in the bowels of the company, meeting with his workers in such places as the assembly line, the warehouse, and the branch offices. To make these visits personal, the CEO should go by himself or accompanied, at most, by a local general manager and, at most, one other company employee. Walking the line with an entourage of executives doesn't cut it—it's impersonal and could be intimidating. When the CEO of a large manufacturing company approaches a machinist on a one-to-one basis, however, it's personal and effective. "I hope you don't mind my interrupting your work," the CEO might begin, "but I want you to know your work is appreciated." Later the CEO might ask the machinist for suggestions or if there's anything about the company that needs attention. If the CEO does this in a down-to-earth way, the result will likely be some good information about the company. And all the while the CEO's building goodwill, by showing appreciation for rank-and-file employees.

At company social gatherings, an employee may approach me with a question. "How do you think the present downturn in the economy will affect our company?" or "Say, Dave, will the government cutbacks on spending change the way we do things in our department?" When a topical item is hot, I may be asked the same question over and over by different people. If I answer tersely because I'm tired of repeating myself, the questioner's feelings might be hurt. So each time, I feel obliged to give the same complete answer. I feel sorry for Thelma, standing next to me, hearing me repeat myself again and again. But Thelma is a supportive spouse, and she listens as intently as if it were all new to her.

When I talk one-to-one with somebody, I look the person squarely in the eye, not diverting my attention. No matter how much someone else may be pulling or tugging on me, the person in front of me is my top priority at that moment. I look at people as if an invisible tattoo on their forehead says, "I am a very important person." And it's absolutely true: Everybody is important.

Every human being has uniqueness. Everyone in the company deserves respect, regardless of position. That's why when VIPs visit our company and I give them the Cook's tour, I introduce them to every employee in the workplace, regardless of title. I keep in mind what Jesus told his disciples in Matthew 20:26–28: "Whoever wishes to be great among you must be your servant, and whoever wishes to be first among you must be your slave. Just as the Son of Man came not to be served but to serve, and to give his life a ransom for many."

Jesus teaches us to respect and love everyone, regardless of station. This advice is appropriate everywhere, and at all levels throughout corporate America.

In Luke 22:49–51, shortly before Jesus was seized and taken to the high priests to be tried, he performed a miracle. A soldier drew his sword and cut off the right ear of the slave of a high priest. Jesus stopped to touch the slave's ear and healed him. Here, even while bombarded by hostility, Jesus took time to care for the slave of an adversary who was attempting to arrest him. This is the epitome of showing personal concern for another, even during trepidation and distress. Surely each of us should emulate Jesus' mindfulness of his fellow beings.

NEVER UNDERESTIMATE THE COMPETITION

Whatever your task, put yourselves into it, as done for the Lord and not for your masters.

—Colossians 3:23

They're up three touchdowns at halftime, yet the winning coach's team loses the game. How can that happen? The coach is so confident of his lead that he refuses to alter his game strategy. The opposing team's coach, however, devises a new game plan for the second half. The game flip-flops and it's called a change in momentum. What really happened is a classic example of underestimating the competition. As in all competitive arenas, it's important to remember that the other guy can think too.

In business, when your marketing strategy is successful in capturing market share, don't believe that the other guy's going to lie down and let you steamroll him. He may emulate your strategy, and he'll probably add a few improvements. He'll do his best to take customers away from you–particularly the ones that you took from him. Just when you think you're so far ahead of the pack you can coast–boy, are you in for a big awakening.

In Samuel 17:43–44, Goliath was convinced he was facing an unworthy opponent. He belittled David and shouted at him, "Am I a dog that you come to me with sticks?" The Philistine cursed David and said he would give his flesh to the birds and wild animals. The cocksure nine-foot warrior knew he could easily slaughter the small shepherd boy, so he let down his guard. Then, with a single stone flung by his slingshot, David slew the awesome giant. Goliath had grossly underestimated his opponent.

In years past, giant corporations held a tremendous advantage over their small competition, in part because the cost of technology was so immense. Today, however, with the advent of the Internet, the small mom-and-pop operation has access to systems that enable it to do business around the globe. Computers that once cost several million dollars and occupied the space of an entire room now sell for a thousand dollars and fit in a backpack. What's more, these tiny brains have far more capacity than the million-dollar-plus mammoths of yesteryear. Consequently, the playing field has been leveled, which allows the small company to compete with the big boys. Today's small company is technology-savvy and light on its feet, capable of turning on a dime. This is no time for WWT or any big company to become complacent, thinking that its sheer size will scare off its smaller competitors.

With Thelma there to quote from the Scriptures about how people become haughty before the fall, I have never let a business success go to my head or felt self-contented. One of the best examples of complacency in the annals of American business is the loss of dominant market share suffered by General Motors, Ford, and Chrysler in the 1970s. Literally hundreds of automakers have come and gone since the "horseless carriage" hit the road at the beginning of the twentieth century. However, this trio, known as the Big Three–Goliaths in their own right–not only survived the fierce early competition, but in the process became the dominating force of American industry as a whole. By the 1950s, the well-being of the U.S. economy rested on the good fortune of these three corporate giants. The prosperity of mighty industries such as iron, steel, rubber, glass, and aluminum revolved around the production of Detroit-made automobiles and trucks. Nearly one out of every five jobs in America was directly or indirectly dependent on either the production or sale of products made by these three companies. In short, the manufacturing of cars was indispensable to the welfare of the entire nation. The car was king. And as the American economy went, so went the world economy.

It was a time when bigger meant better in America because bigger cars meant more prestige. The cars were heavy and bulky. And they were gas-guzzlers. That didn't seem to matter because energy was cheap. By the early 1970s, Americans, an estimated 5 percent of the world's population, drove nearly 40 percent of the world's motor vehicles. There were 120 million cars on the road in the United States. On October 6, 1973, the eve of Yom Kippur, the most holy day of the Jewish religion, Egypt attacked Israel, and for the third time since World War II, the small Jewish state defeated an enemy that greatly outnumbered her. The defeat humiliated the entire Arab world, which retaliated with its most powerful weapon: an oil boycott, aimed primarily at the United States, Israel's staunch supporter. By early January 1974, Americans were lined up bumper to bumper to purchase gasoline. Long lines also appeared outside showrooms at automobile dealerships, as drivers sought subcompacts, in particular, fuel-efficient models equipped with stick shifts. Then, *screech.* Gas prices leveled off at 60 cents per gallon, and a fickle America abruptly became disenchanted with little cars and went back to big, bulky gas-guzzlers. Soon, smaller models were selling only with sizable rebates.

In 1978, the Ayatollah Khomeini seized control of Iran and the Shah of Iran was thrown out. The Ayatollah showed his contempt for the United States by denouncing everything connected with the Western world, and in 1979, he turned off the spigot and created a second oil crisis. In a matter of weeks, gas prices doubled. By spring, Americans were again in long lines at the gas pumps. This time, service stations were unable to satisfy the demand, and many closed on weekends. Americans began forming car pools, and in some areas they were limited to purchasing gasoline only on certain days of the week. Again, gasoline prices soared.

History repeated itself, and overnight there was a demand for small cars. And once again, the domestic automakers did not have them. However, this time a large supply of Datsuns, Hondas, and Toyotas were available to meet the tremendous demand for fuel-efficient cars. The Japanese had huge inventories of small cars and light trucks and, practically overnight, American car buyers were heading to their dealership showrooms. Japanese cars offered not only excellent fuel economy and improved quality, but also threw in many of the features of big cars. At the same time, the quality of American cars had actually slipped a few notches in the late 1970s, as domestic manufacturers struggled to meet new fuel economy and emission standards. It was no contest. The Japanese cars sold like hotcakes and, to the delight of their purchasers, they were good cars, with far fewer problems than those made in the United States. The Big Three were on their knees. Chrysler sought aid from the government, and only with federal financing was the company able to survive. Ford had planned to seek government aid too, but Chrysler beat it to the punch. The Big Three lost huge market share that they have never been able to regain.

Goliath is not the only one who ever fell victim to underestimating the competition. It is an age-old malaise in the world of business. And so is complacency, that insidious disease companies suffer when they become so successful that management ceases to be aggressive. All the while, the small entrepreneur remains hungry and eager to make his mark. As long as aggressive upstarts exist–and they always will–tried and true firms must stay on top of their game.

I constantly remind my managers: You'd be surprised who might come along and take our customers away. What about the competitor who is struggling along, seemingly on the brink of bankruptcy? He's still a contender. Sometimes a competitor down for the count, desperate to survive, attempts something new and untried–something revolutionary–and it's a home run. Difficult times stimulate people to think outside the box. People whose backs are against the wall may take an offensive position they might not have considered earlier. Look for a desperate competitor to start slashing prices and offering deals at bargain prices, or to bring in a new management team to turn the company around. When a competitor looks to be on his last leg–don't be so quick to count him out!

There is no resting on laurels in our competitive world of business. For example, a retailer with dominant market share shouldn't say, "Business is great, so let's reduce our remodeling and advertising expenses to enhance our bottom line. Then we'll really make the big bucks." Seeking short-term gains over long-term profits may drive customers from the store who will never come back. What if the NFL coach who wins the Super Bowl decides, "We've got the best team in football, so this next season, we're not going to recruit new players. We'll stay with the team that won it all this season." Meanwhile, the other teams are recruiting and getting stronger. You know what happens. The following year, that Super Bowl championship team doesn't even make it to the playoffs.

I try to learn from the experience of other businesses, but ultimately the Bible has been my most helpful business manual. Avis Car Rental in its long-popular advertising campaign kept telling us, "We're Number Two, so we try harder." While the Avis slogan received a lot of attention, our goal shouldn't be directed at beating number one. Our goal is to please God. As we are reminded in Colossians 3:23, "Whatever your task, put yourselves into it, as done for the Lord and not for your masters." Here, we are told to do our best to excel in all endeavors as if we are working for God. In this context, "master" is interchangeable with "employer," as well as with "customer" and "vendor." As an employee, failure to do your best could lead to losing a sought-after promotion, or even your job. As a business owner, a weak performance can result in losing customers to the competition. There can be no compromise on quality and you must continue to strive for constant improvement. If you don't keep moving forward, the competition will pass you up, leaving you far behind in its dust.

35

EMPOWERMENT

Without counsel, plans go wrong, but with many advisors they succeed.

—Proverbs 15:22

A wonderful story about empowerment in the Book of Daniel tells about Nebuchadnezzar's dream. Nebuchadnezzar was the powerful king of Babylon who conquered Jerusalem. During the second year of his reign, the king was troubled by a dream and commanded his magicians, enchanters, sorcerers, and four of his wisest advisors–Daniel, Hananhiah, Mishael, and Azariah–to tell him its meaning. The king issued a public decree that his wise advisors would tell him both the dream and its interpretation, and if they could not, they would be torn limb from limb and their houses destroyed. However, if they succeeded in interpreting the dream, they would receive immense riches and honor. When Nebuchadnezzar was told that no mortal could meet his demands, he decreed that all the wise men of Babylon be executed.

Daniel approached the king, requesting time to return with a proper interpretation of his dream. That night, the mystery of the king's dream was revealed to Daniel in a vision, and he blessed God for giving him the answer. Prior to giving his interpretation,

Daniel told the king that wise men, enchanters, magicians, and diviners could tell the meaning of his dream. However, God in heaven can reveal mysteries, and he has disclosed to King Nebuchadnezzar what will happen at the end of days. Then Daniel explained the meaning of the dream. Elated by Daniel's interpretation, the king gave him many splendid gifts and also made him ruler over the whole province of Babylon as well as placing him in charge of all the wise men of Babylon.

Throughout the Bible, story after story of empowerment tells an enlightening lesson teaching us about increased potential through the combined efforts of many. For example, Moses followed the advice of his father-in-law, Jethro, who told him to look for able men among the Israelites who could serve as officers over small and large groups of people. And God empowered Noah to build the ark. Still more remarkable examples of empowerment appear in the First Testament following the Song of Solomon. These are the chronicles of the prophets, some of whom are not well known. Each was empowered by God to interpret his actions in the events of history. These sixteen prophets, from Isaiah through Malachi, were charged with the assignment to keep alive the memory of the Exodus, reinterpret the ancient faith for new times, and proclaim God's will in national crises. After the national disasters of the fall of Israel (722 B.C.) and Judah (598–586 B.C.), the prophets began to speak words of hope and comfort.

The assignments of these prophets and places where they spread the Word of God varied. For instance, Amos preached on social justice, Hosea likened God and Israel to a marriage, Isaiah counseled royalty, and Micah denounced injustice.

Jeremiah talked of new beginnings, Joel called for repentance,

Haggai and Zechariah talked about God as a keeper of promises. Each prophet covered a different department, you might say. All together, they covered a lot of territory.

All sixteen prophets were empowered by God to spread the Word. Their missions continued for about three hundred years, although the precise chronological dates are unknown. Each of the prophets received visions from God; the story of each of their lives and their messages appear in individual books of the Old Testament. Much like the twelve disciples who served Jesus, the prophets in the Old Testament were fully committed to their work. In a time when freedom of speech was not the rule of the day, each put his life in peril by spreading the Word.

Centuries later, Jesus empowered his disciples to carry on the gospel. A leader who developed his management team, Jesus spent three years preparing the disciples for their mission. Like an astute CEO, Jesus handpicked the twelve members of his team based on the special skills of each one that complemented the talents of other team members. Jesus then empowered his disciples to spread the Word, each traveling in a different direction. Jesus trusted them, believed in them, and loved them. And they trusted him, believed in him, and loved him. Jesus taught us that by empowering others, we empower ourselves.

As a CEO, I empower my people because, simply put, I can't be everywhere–at every meeting or on every sales call. With more than five hundred people in this organization, I entrust many individuals with responsibilities ranging from finance operations to customer service, from human resources to information technology. I believe the key to empowerment is trusting people. They have my full support. Many business owners find this hard to do, especially a founder who thinks of the company as his "baby." But my company is not *my* baby, it's *our* baby. You have to let go! To grow, a business owner must empower, develop, and nurture people. I am mindful of what is said in Proverbs 15:22: "Without counsel, plans go wrong, but with many advisors they succeed." Entrepreneurs who fail to empower people will not make the transition from a small start-up company to a large enterprise. As I previously stated, it takes a different set of skills to operate a big company than it does a small company. If a business is to grow, empowerment is essential. Pat them on the back and let them go.

I believe that building and maintaining an entrepreneurial spirit differentiates our company from the competition. As an example of what we do, our sales consultants are empowered to use their discretion to set up Enterprise Resource Planning systems (ERP) for customers. (An ERP is a software program that manages and integrates business processes across multiple divisions and organizational boundaries within a single enterprise.) Now there's no one right way to implement a back-office ERP. While there is a basic plan, different companies have different needs, so every ERP is tailor-made for each customer. Our sales consultants have latitude to make decisions in the field. They're empowered to do what they think is appropriate–they aren't required to continually touch base with us for clearance. What we do ask is that they do what they think serves the best interests of the client and of the company. As it almost always seems to turn out, the decisions they make are the right ones. Empowered to make decisions on their own, they emulate doctrine deeply ingrained in the culture of our organization. The result is good decisions made by people who are not even in management positions. They also gain valuable experience that grooms them for bigger challenges.

Empowering our people has significantly contributed to our company's growth. In addition to building their confidence, it makes them feel they can make a difference in how the customer is served. Our team spirit assures that no one wants to let the team down, and drives everyone to do their best work. As a team member each individual makes his or her contribution, and together we succeed.

36

HAVING A CONTINGENCY PLAN

In speaking of a "new covenant," he has made the first one obsolete. And what is obsolete and growing old will soon disappear.

—Hebrews 8:13

In Genesis 2, God warned Adam not to eat the forbidden fruit. The Lord gave Adam permission to eat all other fruit in the Garden of Eden, but told Adam that the day that he ate from the Tree of the Knowledge of Good and Evil, he would die. Adam, however, having been given free will from the Lord, did eat the fruit given to him by Eve, as did she, claiming that the serpent tricked her.

Although God had told Adam that if he ate the fruit, he would die that same day, because of his love for man, he changed his mind. Instead, he came up with the contingency plan and from that day forth, Adam (man) would work the soil of the land until his body was buried in the ground because "you are dust, and to dust you shall return."

Just as God's contingency plan held Adam and Eve responsible for the "original sin" but did not smite them, there are times in business when a contingency plan requires change–sometimes change that can set a company on an entirely different course.

My original company audited overcharges for customers of railroad companies. Later we changed our business plan to include auditing undercharges for railroad companies themselves. Still later, we concluded our core business shouldn't only be providing auditing service to railroad-related businesses. Why limit our market? We were really in the information technology business on behalf of many types of businesses–and we use technology to change the way those customers do business. Then we rewrote our business plan again, and by 1995 our contingency plan demanded we move from using standard accounting software systems to whole enterprise, resource-planning systems that touch every part of our business. From that, we built slide-chain management systems enabling us to meet the demands of our current customers. So while our original plan didn't specifically foresee the sizable investments we ultimately put into our current systems, our investments anticipated our customers' future needs. Competitors in our industry that did not anticipate altering their original game plan are now having to paddle double-time to meet the needs and demands of their customers in today's market. Right now, we're benefiting from the execution of a contingency plan we initiated years ago.

We have a vertical marketing strategy that serves Fortune 500 companies; simultaneously, we sell IT equipment to the federal government. Our product line meets the demands of the Department of Defense (DOD), which has an enormous need for security and integrated communications systems. With our own systems in place, we are able to serve different DOD agencies such as the

CIA, National Security Agency, the FBI, and the Armed Forces, providing them with better ways to communicate and share information with one another. It's well-known that a company must adjust its modus operandi to comply with government procedures. We knew this going in and understood what we'd have to do. It's what you do if you want business with the government. The potential for huge volume makes it worthwhile. Then, once you get the business, you anticipate that the government is always making changes and you're willing to make changes to accommodate it. In addition to changes occurring in technological uses, as a matter of course, the government makes changes in its contracting methods. So here too, to be in compliance, a government contractor must adapt. Many companies view those changing rules and regulations as too restrictive and won't compete on government contracts.

Our systems run around the clock, every day of the year, because our customers need information at any given moment. So, the very nature of our business requires contingency planning. This means that if a system goes down, we must have an available backup database. So every night, we back up all the data in the systems, which takes three to four hours. As a further safeguard, we store it at an offsite location. Rarely does a system go down, but still, this routine is necessary to our daily contingency plan.

Both internal and external causes can necessitate contingency plans. Internally, a contingency plan could kick in due to turnover of personnel, restatement of earnings by the accounting department, and so on. External causes run the gamut: acts of war, terrorism, change in governmental policy, loss of a major customer, change in economic conditions, trends, and, of course, the competition, which is a moving target.

Ever since the original sin, accounts of contingency plans appear throughout the Bible. For example, in Genesis 41, the Pharaoh dreamed of seven sleek, fat cows and seven ugly, thin cows; and he had a second dream of seven ears of grain, plump and good, growing on a single stalk, and seven thin ears. Joseph was asked to interpret the meaning of the two dreams. He told Pharaoh, "Your dreams were one and the same and God has revealed what he is about to do. The seven good cows are seven fruitful years, and the seven good ears are seven fruitful years. The seven lean and ugly cows and the seven thin ears are seven years of famine. God is telling you that there will be seven years of great plenty throughout all the land of Egypt. They will be followed by seven years of famine that will consume the land. The dream was also telling you to select a discerning and wise man to place in charge of the pending crisis. You should appoint overseers that will store one-fifth of the grain that is produced during the prosperous years and use it as a reserve for the seven years of famine that will befall the land of Egypt."

After his dream interpretation, Joseph was hailed as the most discerning and wise man in the land, so the Pharaoh appointed him second-in-command. Upon accepting his high post, the thirty-year-old Joseph set up a contingency plan. A great famine did follow the seven years of plenty, yet the land of Egypt prospered, using the stored grain to feed its people and sell to other nations. Today's business leaders may lack Joseph's skill in interpreting dreams, but during prosperous business cycles, they can still put contingency plans in place in anticipation of a change in the economy.

I could have taken money out of my business during periods of prosperity, but like Joseph, I kept investing earnings into upgrading our systems, which today are second to none. Recently, a decision was made to put our company in a position where we'd have the capacity to bring certain efficiencies to our customers and partners, while simultaneously driving down their costs. In this effort, our upgrades began to show their merit. Had we stuck to our original plan, we wouldn't enjoy our present competitive edge.

Oftentimes when business is on the skids, companies without a prearranged contingency plan simply react and implement drastic cost-cutting measures. To reduce overhead, employees are laid off, research and development is curtailed, advertising is decreased, expansion plans are canceled, and so on. While pulling in the reins may have merit, reactions of this nature are often short-term fixes that stunt future growth. They can even precipitate the slow death of a company. A company, for example, that lays off people and cuts back on technology spending risks putting itself at a competitive disadvantage when economic conditions improve. It can get so far behind the competition that it never gets back in the running.

To avoid putting ourselves in a position where drastic cost cutting is mandatory, our company has diversified its client base so we're not overly dependent upon a particular industry. For example, in our early stages, our prosperity rested solely on the fate of the railroad industry. Then there was a time when a high percentage of our customers were in telecommunications. Today, our client base is spread out; we have several government contracts, including ones with the Department of Defense, Department of Agriculture, Transportation Security Agency, General Services Administration, Small Business Administration, Federal Communications Commission, and others. Here too, if we put all our eggs in one basket with only federal government contracts, there would be times when spending cuts would be devastating. So for any company that specializes in one area, I recommend devising a contingency plan to keep it from depending on one particular industry. Currently, we're starting to do business with domestic automakers, also a cyclical industry. Here too, we move with caution. While we seek a diverse range of customers, our contingency plan prevents one market segment from becoming a disproportionate percentage of our customer base.

Because God loves man, there are many examples in the Bible that demonstrate that he had contingency plans in place on our behalf. For example, in Deuteronomy 29 Moses commanded the people of Israel to enter into a solemn covenant with God, which is known as the old covenant, based on laws he had received from God. From this "old" covenant, sometimes called a testament, comes the name of the first part of the Bible. Jesus' death on the cross established the new covenant or testament. As it is told in Mark 14:24, "He said to them, 'This is my blood of the covenant, which is poured out for many. Truly I tell you, I will never again drink of the fruit of the vine until that day when I drink it new in the kingdom of God.' " In Romans 10, Jesus says that "the word is near you, on your lips and in your heart."

The old covenant was rigid and based upon absolute adherence to laws, including rituals pertaining to mundane acts like washing and cooking. The individual was also dependent on the holiness of the high priests. The new covenant simply yet elegantly states that your belief must be real and come from your heart, and you must orally express your belief in God and his son, Jesus. You must be committed to your belief and you must live by it. As it is written about God in Hebrews 8:13: "In speaking of 'a new covenant,' he has made the first one obsolete. And what is obsolete and growing old will soon disappear."

Much as the new covenant replaced the formerly sacred old covenant, current circumstances can necessitate a new contingency plan to replace a long-established business plan.

IT'S ABOUT TIME

For everything there is a season, and a time for every matter under heaven:
a time to be born, and a time to die;
a time to plant, and a time to pluck up what is planted;
a time to kill, and a time to heal;
a time to break down, and a time to build up;
a time to weep, and a time to laugh;
a time to mourn, and a time to dance;
a time to throw away stones, and a time to gather stones together;
a time to embrace, and a time to refrain from embracing;
a time to seek, and a time to lose;
a time to keep, and a time to throw away;
a time to tear, and a time to sew;
a time to keep silence, and a time to speak;
a time to love, and a time to hate;
a time for war, and a time for peace.

—Ecclesiastes 3:1–8

Time is precious and we must use it wisely.

I remember waking up on the morning of my twenty-fifth birthday and thinking to myself, "Here I am, a quarter of a century old, and what have I accomplished with my life?"

I wasn't feeling good about myself that day. I thought about the little job experience I had. That was depressing. I realized I had taken from the community without giving much in return. All I had done was take up space. Then the thought came: What if I were to suddenly die? The truth flashed through my mind that I hadn't fulfilled my purpose to God. I had not made a difference in making the world a better place. I vowed that I would not let the next twenty-five years go by and wake up when I was fifty feeling the same way.

Knowing we have a finite amount of time in this world, we should strive to do the best with the time we do have. I look at it this way: God blesses each of us with 86,400 seconds a day. What if each of those seconds was worth a dollar that you could spend any way you wanted, but what you didn't spend was taken away at the end of the day? Certainly, you'd be more careful with your spending, not wanting to waste any of your money. We should think about our time on earth the same way; after all, it's a special gift that God has blessed us with.

In Exodus 16, a story is told about Moses and the Israelites. Forty-five days after their departure from Egypt, the people had become disenchanted and accused Moses of bringing them into the wilderness just so he could kill them with hunger. They complained that they would have been better off never leaving the land of the Pharaohs. Not wanting the Israelites to starve, God made rain from heaven and manna grew from the earth. He did so with the provision that each day the people would gather enough for that day. God would test them to see whether they would follow his instructions. It perplexed the Israelites to see manna on the ground, and Moses explained to them that God had provided enough for each person to eat only what he or she could consume in a single day. "Do not gather more than you need," he told them. He instructed that an omer (an ancient Hebrew dry measure equal to 3.7 quarts, or a little less than a gallon) would be sufficient. Some of the Israelites did as they were told while others gathered more than they required. Moses said to them, "Let no one leave any of it over until morning," but they didn't listen. It did no good to gather too much bread, however, because by the next morning it bred worms, became foul, or simply melted in the sun.

It was wasteful for anyone to take more than he or she could eat because the manna was inedible the following morning. Like uneaten manna, unused time is wasted.

In business, to quote a popular axiom, "time is money." Due to many variables, it's difficult to put an exact value on time, but for the most part, it can be approximated. For example, a salaried worker's time can be measured by dividing his total yearly compensation package by the number of hours he works per annum. Likewise, we convert monetary costs to hourly costs for equipment, rental leases on real estate property, a hotel room for a night's lodging, and so on. While I am not suggesting you break down the cost of everything, it is good to be aware of what time is worth, and more important, to respect every minute.

An employee has an obligation to give a fair day's work for a fair day's pay. When employees tend to personal matters on company time, they are being paid for time they did not work. The same is true about employees who are continually tardy for work, take extended lunch breaks, leave the office early, have long personal conversations on the phone, send personal e-mail letters, and so on. The same individual who wouldn't consider stealing supplies from an employer, may forget that stealing time from an employer is also wrong. While the intent may not be to steal, using company time for personal activities is tantamount to taking money out of the cash register.

At WWT, we're in the business of saving time for our customers. This is what we do. What we bring to the table are ways to enhance our customers' ability to increase efficiency. It all boils down to saving them time. At the end of the day, if the value proposition we propose doesn't give them a return on their investment that translates into saving their time and passing that savings on to their customers, we have nothing to sell. For example, we give our customers access to instantly visible information, and we provide matrixes relative to how various vendors and partners are performing. This information helps them make quick decisions and enables them to determine which vendors and partners are appropriate to do business with. Our competitive edge rests on our ongoing capability to shorten the time it takes the IT products and services we provide to get to market.

Let us remember that a common denominator of today's Internet, new technology, and myriad of applications is focused on one thing: *time.* It's all about improving people's lives with more efficient ways to use their time. This is what the Internet does–you can communicate with people all over the world in a matter of seconds. Likewise, today you can instantaneously obtain information that previously took hours–if it was even obtainable at all. Transactions made via the Internet formerly required considerably more time. Cell phones also conserve our time. I save hours every month by making phone calls while driving, waiting at airports, and so on. And voicemail saves time because you can leave a message and eliminate phone tag.

Those of us who place a high value on our own time should respect other people's time, too. In business, this means being punctual. Being late for an appointment is inconsiderate because it wastes other people's time. So does putting people on hold during a telephone conversation or not calling in advance with a message that you're running late. It is also inconsiderate of other people's time when a cell phone is left on during meetings, or worse, used during a meeting. In my role as CEO, I lead by example, doing my best to always be prompt for meetings and to not keep anyone waiting. My appreciation for time is also exhibited by my discipline in maximizing the use of my own time. Good time management is determined, in part, by being focused. And being focused requires good planning. Here, having a wonderful executive assistant is crucial. I do and, boy, do I appreciate mine.

Good time management means getting the most out of your time. For instance, a young man recently told me he spends three hours every Saturday doing paperwork while his neighbors do lawn work. "I pay $10 an hour to have my grass cut," he explained to me. "Since my time is worth five times that, I'm ahead of the game by applying that time to my career. Now, Dave, if I enjoyed lawn work, it would be a different matter, but the truth is, I don't!" This thinking is perfectly logical. In the workplace, for instance, a good leader wouldn't ask a $200-per-hour executive to spend a morning doing work that was the job of a $12-an-hour employee. The same logic applies to whether it's feasible for a highly paid CEO to travel by private jet. It's a matter of how much his time is worth versus the cost of a private jet.

Time is sometimes squandered due to haste. A person in a hurry may make a mistake that requires additional time to fix. So sometimes, you must pace yourself: Don't rush through a project in a hurry to get the job done. As we are told in Proverbs 13:11: "Wealth hastily gotten will dwindle, but those who gather little by little will increase it."

The Bible makes many references to Jesus' excellent time management. This is evidenced by the magnitude of his accomplishments during the brief three years he had to minister. He devoted his time to ministering to his disciples and to others by example. Also, much of his time was spent healing the sick and healing others spiritually. And when Jesus spoke, he said what he had to say in only a few words–and yet so elegantly.

While Jesus valued his time, he also taught us that we should never be so busy that we neglect each other. His deeds confirm that there are circumstances when we must put aside pressing matters to serve others. Scripture in Matthew 9:18–26 illustrates how Jesus took time to care for a sick woman while he was on his way to the home of a prominent synagogue leader whose daughter had just died. The woman, who had been suffering from hemorrhages for twelve years, thought by touching his cloak she would be healed. When Jesus saw her, he said, "Take heart, daughter; your faith has made you well." The woman instantly recovered.

Here we learn a valuable lesson about time: No matter how busy we are, we must not be so engrossed in our work that we neglect each other. Although our work is important, we should always allocate time for loved ones–our spouses, children, aged parents, and friends.

38

BE FLEXIBLE

And the Lord changed his mind about the disaster he planned to bring on his people.

—Exodus 32:14

The episode of the Golden Calf in Exodus 32 depicts both rigidity and flexibility. While Moses was on his way down from the mountain with the Ten Commandments, the Israelites had become impatient in his absence. So what did they do? They reverted back to their old ways just as when they lived in Egypt. Showing no appreciation for their newfound freedom and all they had received from God, they constructed a gold statue to worship.

God was indeed angry, but he was open to Moses' plea for the Israelites' redemption. Moses implored the Lord to give them another chance. Moses reasoned with God that he had brought his people out of the land of Egypt, and now, if he were to deny them, the Egyptians would say that he did so with evil intent. The Egyptians would say God had planned to kill the Israelites in the mountains and eradicate them from the face of the earth. Hence, Moses pleaded with God to change his mind. Moses also reminded God about how he swore to Abraham, Isaac, and Israel, telling them that he would multiply their descendents like the stars of heaven and that their descendents would inherit a promised land. "And the LORD changed his mind about the disaster that he planned to bring on his people," we read in Exodus 32:14. What better lesson on flexibility than one taught by the almighty?

Business, like all walks of life, is ever-changing and requires adaptability. Our free enterprise system is grounded on our capacity to change: Those who adjust to new ways thrive; those who resist change are soon gone. God has endowed us with a venturesome spirit so that we extend ourselves to face exciting challenges awaiting us. Today's competitive marketplace is no place for the faint of heart. We either move forward or we fall backward. There is no middle road. Indecisiveness is a curse. To make no decision is to make a wrong decision. In the case of the Golden Calf, God was merciful and gave the Israelites a second chance. In business, there may not always be a second chance.

My company has had its share of ups and downs. So far, during the down periods, we've not only survived, we've become stronger. I attribute this, in part, to a weeding-out process that separates the flexible people from the rigid people. Creative people, who are always seeking solutions to new challenges, stay with us. Tough times push everyone to exert himself. Anyone who can't take the heat gets out of the kitchen and seeks a career elsewhere. Competition forces us–and every business–to continually evaluate our entire organization to see where the fat needs to be cut. During these times we search for answers to difficult questions. Is this person productive? Does she bring value? Has he come up with new and better ideas to improve how we do business? We are compelled to take a second look at the kind of talent we have in the organization. Tough times require tough decisions by management, which may lead to thinning out the ranks, moving out people who might have been kept during more prosperous times. It's survival of the fittest, and the end result is a leaner and better organization. Flexible people stay; rigid people leave.

In Matthew 12:10–14, Jesus teaches a lesson about flexibility when he visits a synagogue and comes across a man with a withered arm. The members of the congregation questioned Jesus if it was lawful to cure on the Sabbath. The question was asked to test Jesus. He replied with a question: "Suppose one of you has only one sheep and it falls into a pit on the Sabbath; will you not lay hold of it and lift it out? How much more valuable is a human being than a sheep!" "So is it lawful?" the man with the withered arm asked. Jesus told him to stretch out his hand, and when the man did, his arm was no longer withered. Here, Jesus demonstrates that we must not always cling to traditions and old ways–we must be flexible and make adjustments to fit new occasions. So often people do the same thing over and over again, never giving any thought to trying a new way. Then when somebody dreams up an innovation, they reply, "If it ain't broke don't fix it." Now there's a response that will send a company down the road to obsolescence.

In the Book of Ruth, there is the beautiful story about Ruth, a model of flexibility. Ruth's mother-in-law, Naomi, had lost her two sons. A widow herself, Naomi thought it in the best interests of her two daughters-in-law, Ruth and Orpah, for them to return to their own people. Before bidding them farewell, Naomi thanked them for being such good wives to her sons and such good daughters-in-law. At first both women refused to leave their caring, elderly mother-in-law, but Orpah was finally persuaded and bid her farewell. Ruth did not, and Naomi insisted that she do as Orpah had done. Ruth answered: "Do not press me to leave you or to turn back from following you! Where you go, I will go; where you lodge, I will lodge; your people shall be my people, and your God my God. Where you die, I will die–there will I be buried." Ruth was loyal to Naomi and stayed with her, and the two of them went together to Bethlehem. Unlike Orpah, who obediently did as she was told, Ruth did what she believed in her heart was right. In business, sometimes an employee is given an order but does not feel it is the right thing to do. In such a case, each of us, like Ruth, must speak out and do what we believe is appropriate. We must not be so inflexible that we blindly follow an order even when it goes against our belief system. Submitting to peer pressure and going along with what everyone else does–these are the enemies of flexibility.

The admirable quality of flexibility should be tempered only by adherence to our core principles. Here I refer specifically to the Word of God. As it is written in Hebrews 13:8: "Jesus Christ is the same yesterday and today and forever." Some things never change–they're not supposed to. We should be thankful to God that they don't.

39

YOUR INNER VOICE (THE HOLY SPIRIT)

I hereby command you: Be strong and courageous; do not be dismayed, for the LORD your God is with you wherever you go.

—Joshua 1:9

When people say, "I'm going with my gut instinct," they credit their decisiveness to a whim or impulse. Let's give credit where credit is due. What people call a gut feeling isn't what they think. I believe what we label an innate response is actually spiritually inspired. The above verse, Joshua 1:9, confirms my belief that God is always with me; it is he who guides me, instructing me which way to turn and what to do. God does it through a voice that I hear within myself, even though it has no sound. I hear it because he is guiding me, and if you let him guide you, you will "hear" it and will prosper. You must, however, have unconditional faith in him.

Think about a time you had "instant rapport" with someone. You know, that chemistry that happens between two people when you immediately click. Many happy long-married couples say when they first met it was love at first sight. In business, there are some people whom we meet for the first time and immediately know we will do well by them. Such first impressions happen frequently during sales presentations and job interviews. This is what happened when Jesus selected his disciples, because, as we are told in Matthew 4:18–22, he recruited some of the twelve on the spot. For instance, Jesus recruited his first four disciples while walking by the Sea of Galilee. Jesus saw two fishermen, Peter and his brother, Andrew, who were casting a net into the water, and he called to them, "Follow me, and I will make you fishermen of people." Spontaneously, they dropped their nets and went with him. Then Jesus saw two other brothers, James and John, who were in a boat mending their nets. After calling to them, they too followed him. Jesus' inner voice helped him choose these four men–and seemingly each of them acted on what his inner voice told him.

Then, in Matthew 9:9–13, it is told how Jesus recruited Matthew in much the same manner. Again, Jesus was walking along and saw Matthew sitting at the tax booth. "Follow me," he shouted, and Matthew left the tax booth to join Jesus and the other four men. Peter, Andrew, James, John, and Matthew each made a decision to go with Jesus when there were few who had acclaimed him as the son of God. Still these men willingly abandoned their careers so they could spread the Word of God. Remarkably, they didn't prolong their decision making–they acted spontaneously after only a brief encounter with Jesus.

I listen carefully to my inner voice, particularly during an interview with a prospective employee. Sure, I give credence to what I read in a résumé, because we are constantly reminded in scripture that we will know them by their fruit–meaning that a person's track record speaks volumes. Nonetheless, a job candidate is much more than what appears on a piece of paper. If people were hired based solely on their résumés, there would be no need for interviews. They'd be hired over the Internet. I want to know if a person's heart is in the right place, and only a face-to-face meeting can show this. Just how I evaluate a candidate is a combination of several things: a person's facial expression, tone of voice, eye contact, body language, and so on. I don't look for any particular signal. I can sense a person's integrity and caring nature—my inner voice lets me know. I don't want a person who is on the selfish or greedy side in our organization—no matter how impressive his education or employment background. Sometimes it happens that I get in tune with someone's inner spirit, what I call the essence of a person. When this happens, two people can really connect.

I'm continually looking for people who are caring and enthusiastic. These individuals exude energy and love. I describe this ability as superpower, the Holy Spirit working within a person. I'm convinced this is what our company sells more than anything else—love and energy—so I look for it in the people we hire. Love and energy surface when you have complete faith and confidence in God's Word, when you fully believe in what he can do in your life. You will have an abundance of success, but it's not personal gratification you seek; instead, everything you do is directed to the benefit of others.

Knowing how much faith I place in my inner voice, I respect what others hear from theirs. So when one of our people is filled with enthusiasm and convinced that a project is a winner, I see if we can find a way to let him run with it. Sure, I may have doubts, but I express them by asking sincere questions and then openly listening to explanations. And, as I previously said, it's important to let people take risks, in particular when they're consumed with love and energy. I do this, mindful of the times when I listened to my inner voice despite those people who thought I was moving in the wrong direction or putting the company in jeopardy. For instance, in 1991, we made a decision to focus on doing business with the federal government. At the time, with the exception of a handful of large contractors, very few people in the Midwest were doing government business. Getting into this segment took a lot of time and energy because we had to learn the ropes, build relationships, develop political contacts, and learn the government acronyms, its culture and so forth. I quickly discovered we'd be dealing with people who are the best and brightest individuals in the nation's capital.

Right off the bat, we saw it would require a lot of hard work, but the fact that the federal government was spending $25 billion a year on technology got our attention. We were excited and energized. Every time we met with military personnel, we became exuberant. We thrived on learning their culture, business practices, and contracting processes. We were blessed to have Maureen Brinkley and Debra Diggs, two wonderful friends in the General Services Administration, who coached and advised us. Ron Wicker at the Small Business Administration was another big supporter who worked closely with us.

Still, well-meaning friends were among the first to say that I'd wreck everything we built if the company went after government contracts. However, as I learned in a parable that Jesus told in Matthew 12:3–8, there are times when we must defy conventional thinking. In this parable, Jesus was harshly criticized by the Pharisees for going through the grain fields even though it was the

Sabbath so his disciples could be fed. Jesus recites an incident when David had entered the temple with his companions who were hungry. He told how they ate the bread of the priests, which was also in violation of the law. "Why was what David and his companions did unlawful but lawful for the priests?" Jesus questioned. "Have you not read in the law that on the Sabbath the priests in the temple break the Sabbath and yet are guiltless?" He then challenged the priests not to be so quick to condemn but instead to be merciful.

Jesus listened to his inner voice even when it prompted him to defy authorities. Luke 4:17–24 cites an incident when he faced rejection while visiting Nazareth, the place of his birth. On one Sabbath, he read a portion of the scroll in the synagogue. Upon finishing his reading, he rolled up the scroll and sat down. While the members of the congregation and rabbis were impressed with him, they discarded him because he was the son of Joseph who lived in Nazareth, so how wise could he truly be? Jesus remarked to them, "No prophet is accepted in the prophet's hometown." He also said that God anointed him to bring good news to the poor. When he was finished, an enraged crowd tried to throw him off a cliff, but he escaped.

The local people in my community tried to convince me that an African-American in the Midwest didn't belong in the technology industry. I listened, but didn't heed their comments. The reasons they gave were not good reasons. As far as I was concerned, the color of my skin or where I lived were not valid reasons to stay out of this industry. I read and reread the words of Jesus: "No prophet is accepted in the prophet's hometown." How well I understood this passage. It was as if he had said those words directly to me.

40

PEOPLE WILL SUPPORT WHAT THEY HELP CREATE

For it is written in the law of Moses, "You shall not muzzle an ox, while it is treading out the grain." Is it for oxen that God is concerned? Or does he not speak entirely for our sake? It was indeed written for our sake, for whoever plows should plow in hope and whoever threshes should thresh in hope of a share in the crop.

—1 Corinthians 9:9–10

The above scripture reminds us that just as a farmer feeds a portion of his crop to an ox as it treads out grain, so must we share our dreams and plans with the people working with us. This, I believe, is the best way to win support.

How well successful business leaders know the value of early participation. In any new venture–from a new product to the start-up of a business–success depends on winning ample support. People will be more supportive when invited to participate early on. In contrast, the more time that lapses, the more likely it is that there will be resistance. As I have mentioned in previous chapters, because people feel comfortable with the status quo, they resist change. In particular, they oppose change that they can't control.

Inviting them in during the early stages gives them a say in determining what will be in the future.

Due to the confidentiality surrounding most new projects, it's wise to be selective regarding whom you invite to participate. Recklessness can result in losing an otherwise competitive advantage due to a leak in classified information. For this reason, it's crucial to select only trusted people with proven track records.

A big bonus gained from inviting your people to participate during the conceptual stage is that you gain their support, and equally important, their input. They are supportive, first, because they feel privileged to be included on the ground floor. Simply put, people like being privy to confidential information. Second, they feel ownership in the project because they were there in its infancy–now it's not just your baby, it's "our baby."

When a new idea is introduced in its conceptual stage, getting it to evolve to stage two hinges on its presenter's conviction that it will succeed. The more clearly leaders present their vision, the more likely it will become their people's vision. As we are told in Hebrews 11:1, "Faith is the assurance of things hoped for, the conviction of things not seen." With this in mind, you must share your dream of what is to be. A vision presented in the abstract must ride to its success on enthusiasm and passion. This is what makes it come alive. Your dream becomes *their* dream. Help the dream become real to others. The vision you paint in their minds is like an architect's blueprint. Faith, the assurance of things hoped for, shows your people where they can help flesh out that blueprint.

Here's how this works: One of our departments catered to the telecommunications market. It smoothed out the supply chain, focusing on the delivery of equipment and materials to customers. One of the department's functions was to provide the status of a particular product as it moved along the supply chain to the customer. At the time, nobody offered this service. Our advanced technology allowed customers to take their inherited systems, via the web, to talk and communicate with our systems. This application worked on the supplier side, as well as the customer side. It provided real visibility in real time–24/7–anytime, anywhere in the world. At the time, this was cutting edge in the telecommunications market.

In 1998, we made a decision to spin off the department and create a subsidiary, telcobuy.com. Now this was during the dot-com craze when everyone wanted to invest in B2B (business to business) and e-commerce. However, unlike many of the Internet start-ups, we had a real system that worked; we also had real revenue and real profits. It wasn't like some of those dot-com companies with unproven business plans. A couple of investment bankers talking about doing a public underwriting said that with our revenues, a public offering would mean $1.5 to $2 billion in market capitalization.

To launch telcobuy.com, we knew we'd have to get the buy-in from our entire organization. Why was that? Because we knew people adapt best to change when they're involved at the front end of a new project. We brought folks in during the early decision-making stage, realizing that once telcobuy.com was up and running, it would affect every facet of how we did business. This meant all employees would have to reevaluate their process to adapt to the new way–Julene Tojo in operations, Tom Strunk in accounting, Bob Olwig in marketing, Kurt Grimminger in contract manufacturing–everyone. Every aspect of our business would be woven into this system we were setting up. Once in full swing, telcobuy.com would increase efficiencies throughout our entire organization. We were aware that the systems we were building were difficult for larger organizations to set up because the core business had to buy into it. This meant that if we succeeded, we'd be a giant step ahead of the competition.

To make it work, we wanted everyone's involvement. And to get everyone excited about being involved, we invited participation in each step–the naming of the subsidiary company, its trademark, and even its logo. We were constantly asking our people for their input. "What if we decided to implement this step in your department?" "What are your thoughts on adding that procedure to your staff's routine?" In addition to seeking sound advice, we wanted them to contribute ideas so they'd have ownership in the new venture.

We kept telling our people that once the system was operating, no other company our size could match it. After letting them know it could mean everything to our future, and, most importantly, benefit our customers and vendors, we could feel excitement and enthusiasm in the air.

We constantly communicated every stage of its progress and announced each milestone reached. Then, when telcobuy.com was ready to go, we had a huge party during the Christmas holidays for the entire organization–a real celebration with everyone congratulating one another, hailing it as a team effort. Not surprisingly, telcobuy.com was successful right from the start. No doubt much of the credit goes to the shared passion of the people involved from conception to implementation. Nobody was kept in the dark, not even for a moment–they shared the vision, and that vision became reality. In Proverbs 3:27, it is written: "Do not withhold good from those to whom it is due, when it is in your power to do it." We were determined to include everyone in every stage of telcobuy.com and to make sure they clearly understood that everyone would benefit–the company, the customers, and our vendors.

41

NETWORKING

Whoever welcomes you welcomes me, and whoever welcomes me welcomes the one who sent me. Whoever welcomes a prophet in the name of a prophet will receive a prophet's reward; and whoever welcomes a righteous person in the name of a righteous person will receive the reward of the righteous; and whoever gives even a cup of cold water to one of these little ones in the name of a disciple—truly I tell you, none of these will lose their reward.

—Matthew 10:40–42

The above passage is as appropriate today as it was two millennia ago. If you go to my friend, you will be welcomed as my friend's friend.

It is said that if everyone in America had to start over from scratch–with nothing–the same people who originally had the most money would have it back again within five years. That's based on the premise that they didn't lose their networks or connections.

Those with good reputations would keep their networks. A good reputation and a good network are among the most valuable assets a person can have. Why? Because it opens doors that provide immediate access to otherwise inaccessible people. The very foundation of an effective networking system is one's reputation. My definition of a network begins with all the people you know, and who they know, plus who those people know–and so on. It works on the same principle as a chain letter that's sent out to ten people and then mailed by each recipient to ten more people. Then the one hundred people who receive it repeat the procedure, and it's up to one thousand, then ten thousand–the number grows exponentially. It has been said everyone in the United States is only six people removed from every other person in the United States. It's a matter of asking the right person if he or she knows somebody who knows somebody else.

Let's say, for example, that after I wrote this book, I didn't know anyone in the publishing business. To make that all-important contact with a publisher, the first thing I'd do is carefully think about somebody I knew that had either: 1) written a book, 2) worked for a newspaper or magazine publisher, 3) owned a bookstore, or 4) lived in New York and was well connected with movers and shakers there. If I couldn't identify such a person, I'd call one of my contacts that could. It so happens I know individuals that fall into all four of these categories, and I'd have several irons in the fire simultaneously working on making introductions on my behalf. Had I selected somebody in New York, it would be an individual in a field likely to do business with people in the publishing industry. Or I might have gone with a "well-connected" New Yorker in touch with movers and shakers. Based on past experience, I'm certain that before long I'd be put in touch with several editors, as well as a leading literary agent, who would know key players in New York book publishing circles.

Successful businesspeople in every field network every day, calling on friends, associates, and other contacts who in turn make introductions for them. Bear in mind one important point about networking: A network is only as good as the reputation of each person in it. A network begins with the person who wants an introduction. If that person's not worthy of being introduced–or if the individuals the person contacts are not reputable–it's dysfunctional. The same is true of any link in its chain of people. The chain breaks when someone of poor repute is responsible for making an introduction. Think about it. Of what merit is an introduction from a disreputable person? Why would anyone want to meet somebody recommended by such a person? The source–at any link in the network–is only as strong as the reputation of its weakest link.

In the King James Version of the Bible, we are told in 1 Thessalonians 5:20–22 that we should abstain from all appearance of evil. Here, we are cautioned to be particular about with whom we associate, because we will be judged by the company we keep. There is much truth in the saying "Birds of a feather flock together." This is why Thelma and I recently turned down an invitation to have dinner with friends at one of St. Louis's finer restaurants because it was located on the property of a gambling casino. We were concerned what people might think. Because we don't gamble, we don't want people to see us in that environment. But our concern was not only for ourselves: As the CEO of a company, I have a responsibility to present a good image on behalf of our employees and my community. I've worked very hard building up a good reputation, and I do my best to protect it.

When I first went into business, I called George Craig, senior vice president of marketing at Union Pacific, my mentor during my early days at the railroad. George had been in the business for many years and was one of the most respected individuals in the industry. After I explained my business plan for providing auditing services to railroad companies, George introduced me to many key decision-makers in the industry. Because his reputation was impeccable, the executives he called on my behalf were partially presold on me. They figured, "Anyone George Craig speaks highly of, must be okay." "Whoever welcomes you welcomes me, and whoever welcomes me welcomes the one who sent me."

That's another thing about networking. Be particular about making recommendations to a third party. For instance, had George regularly recommended individuals who didn't pan out, he would have no credibility. But since George believed in me, he was willing to put his reputation on the line along with mine. George was familiar with my track record at Union Pacific, so he felt comfortable opening doors for me. Remember that when you endorse someone, it reflects on you. Of course, when it works, both parties benefit and are grateful to you for bringing them together. This is what makes it all worthwhile.

Another mentor of mine is Luke Fouke, who was my landlord when I first started my company. Over time, we built a close relationship, and he began to introduce me to his friends; many were movers and shakers in St. Louis, including some of the city's most influential bankers. Later, Luke was instrumental in getting my son, David, into Mary Institute/Country Day School and my daughter, Kimberly, into Whitfield, two top private schools in the area. My son made lifelong friends during his school days, and now, ten years later, he's doing some work with one classmate who runs his retired father's media company. This is a good example of how an extended network operates. One door opens to another door to another door, and on and on.

Because my reputation is on the line with the people in my network, I am selective about whom I refer to my contacts. For instance, my coauthor told me that several people call him every month looking for a literary agent. "I'd like to help everyone," Bob explained. "But if I referred every wannabe author to my agent, he'd be bombarded with so many weak book proposals that my recommendation would be worthless. So if I tried to help everyone, I wouldn't be able to help anyone. For this reason, I make sure to read an author's book proposal, and only if I'm convinced it has merit will I forward it to Al." This concurs with my thinking. If I send unqualified people on job interviews to my contacts in high positions, I'll lose my credibility, and when a highly qualified person solicits my assistance, I won't be able to help.

Networking is a two-way street. I've hired many of my top executives after an introduction by someone I admire. For example, we hired a man who was formerly a senior vice president of services at Alcatel, a partner of ours. It was after Alcatel reorganized the entire North American office and wanted to help relocate this man, who was highly respected by their management. Again, it's about reputation–the job candidate's, Alcatel's, and my company's. I'm flattered that the people at Alcatel thought so highly about us that they referred him. Again, it boils down to people wanting to do business with people they like and trust. And they want the people that they like to do business with to do business with other people they like. Based on this premise, we have a program within our organization that relies heavily on our employees referring their friends and family members to us. To make this happen, we provide our employees with an incentive to send people to us by paying a finder's fee after the new person has worked here for a given period of time. This program has been a big success in enhancing our recruiting efforts.

It doesn't necessarily happen quickly, but in time, solid networks are built, and as associates advance in their careers, you're sure to eventually end up with some wonderful contacts in high places. While it's true that coming from a prominent family with prime social ties assures a running head start, Thelma and I made it without those advantages. If you concentrate on building an excellent reputation, in time your network will spread, and before long, you'll be "well connected." Coming from the poor side of town in a small rural community in western Missouri, I am proof that it can happen. My network of people has opened doors in high places, including meetings with U.S. presidents, senators and congressmen, the secretary general of the United Nations, and CEOs of the nation's largest companies.

A strong recommendation from somebody high up, such as one of the above-mentioned VIPs, really gets people's attention. However, one recommendation tops all others. It's told in Matthew 3:16–17, when John the Baptist baptized Jesus: "And when Jesus had been baptized, just as he came up from the water, suddenly the heavens were opened to him and he saw the Spirit of God descending like a dove and alighting on him. And a voice from heaven said, 'This is my Son, the Beloved, with whom I am well pleased.' " How's that for a strong recommendation from a high place.

42

CONVICTION

Blessed are you when people revile you and persecute you and utter all kinds of evil against you falsely on my account. Rejoice and be glad, for your reward is great in heaven, for in the same way they persecuted the prophets who were before you.

—Matthew 5:11–12

Thelma and I recently headed the African-American Leadership Initiative, a fund-raising branch of the United Way in St. Louis. A minimum $1,000 contribution qualified a donor to be a member of the Chapman Society, and those who gave $10,000 became members in the Alexis de Tocqueville Society. In total, the campaign raised $1.45 million, making it the largest African-American Leadership Initiative unit in the country. There were thirty-five donors in our unit who contributed $10,000 or more.

Throughout the campaign, my wife and I spoke at many fund-raising events, and as we commonly do, we quoted biblical scripture and praise. We also mailed letters containing passages from the Bible. Our messages expressed what we believe. We conveyed that much is required from people who have received much. We reminded them that it is more blessed to give than to receive, and we talked about stewardship. While the campaign raised a record amount of money, we received one letter that criticized us. The writer stated that business professionals should not cite scripture or give prayer because it could offend non-Christians. The letter specifically stated I should have been more sensitive to those people in our audience who were Jewish, Muslim, and Hindu.

I read the letter to our Doing Business by the Book Sunday school class. I told them, "There are times when you'll be criticized for spreading the Word of God, and some people won't like you for doing it. But that's okay. We believe others will benefit from learning biblical principles and our message will enrich their lives." I then added, "God blessed us with a successful campaign that helped many people."

Certainly, our intent wasn't to offend; we wanted to serve as an inspiration and share the Word of God. God is with us twenty-four hours a day, and Thelma and I never tune out his presence. Some people think their spiritual beliefs should be separate from their business and public lives. We never leave our beliefs at home.

As it turned out, only a handful of the people involved in the United Way campaign felt affronted. Just the same, Thelma and I would never deny our conviction. How could we, knowing example after example of courageous people in the Bible who refused to compromise their beliefs, even in the face of torture and death. What we did palls by comparison. The vast majority commended our boldness in saying what was in our hearts. And how many times did Jesus demonstrate his faith in God, refusing to renounce his beliefs.

For example, in Mark 14:57–65 there was the time when Jesus was brought before the high priest, all the chief priests, the elders and scribes. This scripture recounts the way Jesus reacted, knowing that the outcome of the trial would determine whether he received a death sentence. False testimony was given by some who said they heard him say that he would destroy the temple and in three days build another, one not made by hands. The high priest asked Jesus to speak in his defense, but he remained silent. When the high priest asked him, "Are you the Messiah, the Son of the Blessed One?" Jesus said, "I am; and you will see the Son of Man seated at the right hand of the Power, and coming with the clouds of heaven." The high priest said to the court, "You have heard his blasphemy! What is your decision?" All of them condemned him to die. Some spit on him. They blindfolded him and struck him, shouting, "Prophesy!" The guards beat him. In the face of death, as he did many times throughout his brief life, Jesus was unbending, refusing to deny his convictions.

Recall the story of Job, who refused to deny his faith in God, even while being subjected to severe pain and loss of his vast wealth. Likewise, Shadrach, Meshach, and Abednego would not bow down to a statue of a gold god, knowing that the penalty meant being burned alive in the king's furnace. One of my favorite passages appears in Matthew 14:3–8 and tells about John the Baptist's refusal to deny his beliefs when imprisoned by King Herod. John had been imprisoned because he stated that it was unlawful for Herod to be with his brother Philip's wife, Herodias. The ruler wanted to execute John, but feared how the crowd would react, since they regarded John as a prophet. At a banquet to celebrate Herod's birthday, the daughter of Herodias danced, and she pleased the king so much that he promised to grant her whatever she might ask. Prompted by her mother, she said, "Give me the head of John the Baptist here on a platter." John the Baptist had known he risked punishment for speaking out against the king's indiscretion. He was right because Herod had John beheaded.

Still another story, known as "The Good Samaritan," that illustrates conviction appears in Luke 10:27–37. Here, Jesus told a group of people that they should love their neighbor "as yourself." A man asked, "Who is my neighbor?" Jesus answered with a parable about a man traveling from Jerusalem to Jericho, who is attacked by robbers. The robbers stripped him of his clothes, beat him, and left him on the road half-dead. By chance, a priest on his way to Jericho passes by, but when he sees the dying man, he goes to the other side of the road to avoid him. Likewise, a Levite passes by and also avoids the dying man. Next a Samaritan passes by and is moved with pity. Stopping to aid the dying man, he pours oil and wine on his wounds and applies bandages. Then the Samaritan puts the dying man on his mule and takes him to an inn for further care. The next day the Samaritan gave two denarii to the innkeeper, and said, "Take care of him; and when I come back, I will reimburse you for your expenses." After completing his parable, Jesus asked: "Which of the three men was a neighbor to the distressed man?" Answering his own question, Jesus continued, "The one who showed him mercy." After a pause, Jesus said, "Go and do likewise."

The priest and the Levite avoided getting involved, because doing what was right meant taking risks. But the stranger stood by his convictions, doing what he knew was right, even though he placed himself in peril. The stranger set an example for each of us to follow. To this day, a person who performs a good deed for a stranger is referred to as a Good Samaritan.

Today, life and death situations rarely test our convictions;

nonetheless, day-to-day challenges in business put us to the test. During an economic downturn, for instance, belt-tightening may be the order of the day. It's always hard to let people go, but sometimes it must be done. If a company doesn't cut back, an entire organization can be placed in jeopardy. In such a scenario, a strong leader must make brutally difficult decisions, because the first obligation is to protect the whole organization. Decisions of this nature are unpopular and certainly not an easy route to turn a business around. This lesson appears in Leviticus 25:3–4: God said to Moses: "Six years you shall sow your field, and six years you shall prune your vineyard, and gather in their yield." Certain branches of a tree must be chosen for pruning so the tree can thrive; similarly, senior management must prune so that their companies may grow stronger. Pruning may also be required with marginal customers. A company may spend too much time with a small account relative to its sales volume, and as a result, neglect major customers. So again, necessary pruning can restore an ailing company to good health. When people are involved, nobody looks forward to pruning; it takes strong conviction to do what's in the vital interest of the organization.

The media seems to thrive on reporting about the greed and corruption of America's business leaders, and while the acts of such individuals are utterly inexcusable, this behavior is not the norm but does make for a titillating story for the evening news. As somebody once said, a man can rob a bank on Main Street and it makes the front page, but nobody ever hears about the sweet old lady on Elm Street who bakes an apple pie for her next-door neighbor. There are, however, thousands of American CEOs who give themselves pay cuts and refuse to take an annual bonus during hard times. Likewise, they don't "cook the books" to meet earnings expectations on Wall Street. Nor do they decrease employee health coverage when premiums skyrocket. These selfless business leaders go to work every morning with a mission to serve their employees, customers, vendors, and shareholders.

What's more, contrary to what the news reports, there are thousands of contractors who win low-bid government contracts without compromising the quality of the work they perform. And there are publishers who stand behind a quality book with an important message, knowing it will never be a best seller, and more probably a financial bust. Also, there are newspaper publishers who delay going to press with a breaking story because it hasn't been accurately fact-checked. There are actors and actresses who turn down parts that pay multimillion salaries for roles that require them to smoke or do nude scenes. Likewise, there are honest auditors who refuse to give a favorable auditing opinion at the risk of losing a corporate client that generates tens of millions of dollars in fees. And attorneys who won't represent an unscrupulous client. These are all examples of men and women with strong conviction—you just never hear about them because they simply do what they're supposed to do and that doesn't sell newspapers.

As we look for people who have conviction in what they do, we can sometimes weed out the undesirable by viewing job histories. For instance, for a few years in the late 1990s, in the search for people with strong IT backgrounds, demand exceeded supply. As a result, to be competitive in the job market, companies had to pay sizeable sign-on bonuses. Some IT people took advantage of the situation, jumping from company to company, collecting one sign-on bonus after another. News of this prompted us to be on the lookout to avoid hiring a "jumper." So our search emphasized loyalty and team spirit, excellent qualities to look for when interviewing job candidates–and that ruled out the jumpers.

One job candidate told me, "I know it was wrong to accept so many sign-on bonuses, but you have to realize what it was like back then. It was part of the IT craze–everybody was doing it."

"Everybody does it" is always a feeble excuse. People with strong conviction stick to their principles and defy conventional thinking. As Jesus tells us in Matthew 5:11–12: "Blessed are you when people revile you and persecute you and utter all kinds of evil against you falsely on my account. Rejoice and be glad, for your reward is great in heaven, for in the same way they persecuted the prophets who were before you."

•

43

HAVING A SUCCESSION PLAN

As for me, this is my covenant with you: You shall be the ancestor of a multitude of nations. No longer shall your name be Abram, but your name shall be Abraham, for I have made you the ancestor of a multitude of nations. I will make you exceedingly fruitful; and I will make nations of you, and kings shall come from you. I will establish my covenant between me and you, and your offspring after you throughout their generations, for an everlasting covenant, be God to you and to your offspring after you. And I will give to you, and to your offspring after you, the land where you are now an alien, all the land of Canaan, for a perpetual holding; and I will be their God.

—Genesis 17:4–8

In this scripture, God initiated a succession plan for Abraham. The Bible, God's will, is his succession plan for us.

In business, a succession plan is also a covenant; it sets forth a leader's responsibilities to employees, vendors, and customers to assure them their future is intact. A succession plan is a commitment that the company will continue under able leadership when the present leader and management team are no longer around. A covenant lets employees know their careers are secure, and assures business partners, vendors, and customers that business will continue as usual in the event of an unexpected (or expected) circumstance. Thus, contracts will be honored, services will continue, and a seamless transition will endure.

For obvious reasons, a succession plan benefits employees—they are unemployed if the company goes out of business. Customers, vendors, and suppliers also have a vested interest—the untimely demise of a major partner or supplier negatively impacts business. I have firsthand knowledge of how they react. Major suppliers and customers have candidly expressed that had my company not had a succession plan, they wouldn't do business with us. Like myself, these companies are interested in establishing long-term relationships with an organization. They don't feel comfortable knowing that if something happened to one individual, the relationship would cease. Rather than being dependent upon a single person, they want assurances that the company will continue to be in good hands.

Key individuals work side by side with me at WWT, and there is a transitional plan in place to run the company in my absence. Telcobuy, our subsidiary company, has its own management team, so, even now, it doesn't require my full-time involvement. A board of directors stands ready to govern the company, and it is structured so my family will have a voice in its guidance. I have sought the counsel of one of St. Louis's largest law firms, to handle my estate planning, so I am confident that my family will also be provided for.

I am aware that some business leaders neglect to plan ahead for the event of their demise, or for that matter, their disability or retirement. In some incidences, a CEO who founded his company thinks he's indispensable and can't be replaced—or invincible, and nothing will ever happen to him. However, nobody is either indispensable or invincible. It's usually a matter of an individual who doesn't want to step down and let others be totally responsible for the management of the organization–because they may actually do a better job. In my opinion, it's an ego problem. You remember: Ego is an acronym for Edging God Out.

Jesus addresses the subject of succession plans in Luke 12:13–21. In this scripture, he tells a parable about a rich man who was worried about not having a place to store his crops. After giving the matter serious thought, the man said, "I will do this: I will pull down my barns and build larger ones, and there I will store all my grain and my goods. Afterward, I will feel secure in having ample goods to last for many years, and I will relax, eat, drink, be merry." But God said to him, "You fool! This very night your life is being demanded of you. And the things you have prepared, whose will they be?" Jesus concludes this parable by saying that those who store up treasures for themselves are not rich toward God. Here, Jesus is telling us to have a contingency plan in place so that we may continue to benefit others long after we are gone. We are also reminded that no one knows when his or her life may end abruptly, so we must prepare in advance for the unforeseen.

In Numbers 20:12, while Moses and Aaron were in the wilderness, God told them that because they did not trust in him to show his holiness before the eyes of the Israelites, they would not bring them into the Promised Land. Moses was 120 years old when he led the Israelites to the banks of the Jordan River; on the other side was the Promised Land. Moses knew that he was not permitted to cross the river to lead the Israelites into the land. Then in Deuteronomy 31:7–8, Moses said to Joshua, "Be strong and bold, for you are the one who will go with this people into the land that the LORD has sworn to their ancestors to give them; and you will put them in possession of it. It is the LORD who goes before you. He will be with you; he will not fail you or forsake you. Do not fear or be dismayed." So here, Moses instructs Joshua to carry out his charge. Although Moses was disappointed that he could not personally carry out his forty-year-old long-term goal, he had peace of mind knowing his succession plan assured that the Israelites would be delivered to the Promised Land.

Matthew 26:26–29 narrates a succession plan delineated by Jesus at the Last Supper. During the meal, Jesus gave a blessing over the bread and said to the disciples, "Take, eat; this is my body." Then he lifted his cup, gave thanks, and told them, "Drink from it, all of you; for this is my blood of the covenant, which is poured out for many for the forgiveness of sins. I tell you, I will never again drink of this fruit of the vine until that day when I drink it new with you in my Father's kingdom." This covenant was Jesus' succession plan, and it has stood the test of time for over two thousand years.

As we learn from the Bible, great nations, as well as today's modern corporations, make covenants to their people. These covenants are designed to secure their future wellness beyond the life of a single individual or group of individuals. Our good principles must be passed down to our children, and in turn, theirs will be passed down to their children.

These wonderful principles are right there in the Word of God. The Bible teaches them to us; this is our inheritance. Likewise, a business built on worthy principles will endure to be passed down to future generations.

44

BLESSED TO BE A BLESSING

I call heaven and earth to witness against you today that I have set before you life and death, blessings and curses. Choose life so that you and your descendants may live, loving the LORD your God, obeying him, and holding fast to him; for that means life to you and length of days, so that you may live in the land that the LORD swore to give to your ancestors, to Abraham, to Isaac, and to Jacob.

—Deuteronomy 30:19–20

We have choices. By opting to believe in God and obeying his commands, we invite God's rich blessings on ourselves; we are obligated, in turn, to pass those blessings on to others. As CEO, my top priority is to serve others. I am privileged and blessed to accept this role.

Serving others is a central theme of our corporate culture. This caring environment tells the organization their employer is driven not by the bottom line, but by doing good for others. Sure, we want to be profitable, for without profits, we can't invest in our future, or for that matter, stay in business. But that's not what drives us. Our purpose is to serve, and when our people know this, they are highly motivated to do their best work. We want them to receive the satisfaction of knowing they are making a difference.

Around here, we feel that we are blessed in order that we may be a blessing–blessed to be a blessing.

The Scriptures teach us to look out for one another. Starting with Matthew 25:31, Jesus describes a time in the future when he will sit on a throne in heaven surrounded by angels. At such time, all the nations will be gathered before him, and he will separate people as a shepherd does when he pilots sheep to the right and goats to the left. In Matthew 25:34–40, Jesus' vision continues when he tells the kindness he received from mankind. He talks about how he was given food when he was hungry; how he was given beverages when he was thirsty. He describes how he was a stranger and people welcomed him; he was naked and was given clothing; he was sick and taken care of; he was imprisoned and was visited. "Truly I tell you," Jesus expresses, "just as you did it to one of the least of these who are members of my family, you did it to me."

In this scripture, Jesus' message is that we should care for each other as we would for him–he excludes no one! Often people forget to apply what Jesus teaches in this passage to the workplace. We may realize that we should care for the thirsty, the hungry, and the sick, but the extent of our caring should not stop with those who are in dire need. We must adhere to his teachings in our daily dealings with coworkers, customers, vendors–everyone. We do it because it's right. We may be the "only Bible" they see that day. There shouldn't be an ulterior motive; profit takes a back-seat to caring about others. Don't expect payback. Our reason for caring is because God asked us to care. We are here to serve, not to be served. That is our charge–we are blessed to be a blessing. Every morning of my life, I am excited to get out of bed, knowing I can bless other human beings in my walk today.

How blessed you are when you care for others, knowing that because God lives in them, you are blessing the Lord. Our many other blessings include all the wonderful things we have: family, opportunities, freedom. Life is a blessing. People often express pride in what they have: "I'm proud to be an American," "My little girl is my pride and joy." However, several scriptural references on the subject of pride advise us that pride is an undesirable quality. In Proverbs 16:18, for instance, we are reminded that pride is followed by destruction, and a haughty spirit is followed by a fall. And in 2 Corinthians 10:17–18, we are told: "Let the one who boasts, boast in the Lord. For it is not those who commend themselves that are approved, but those whom the Lord commends."

So what ought we to say to express these feelings of joy? Give credit to God. Whenever you are tempted to credit luck, good genes, or personal contacts, remember that he has blessed you, so consider your every blessing as a gift from God. Learn to say, "I am blessed to be an American, and live in a land where I have freedom." Concerning your exceptional children, you might say, "I am blessed to have wonderful children." Likewise, when you enjoy good health, instead of knocking on wood, give credit to the Lord by saying, "I am blessed with good health." Nor should you credit good fortune for your dream job. Better you should say, "God has blessed me with an excellent job." When you do this, you are exalting God. Never forget that he is the source of all your blessings.

45

A SUPPORTIVE SPOUSE

He who finds a wife finds a good thing, and obtains favor from the LORD.

—Proverbs 18:22

King Solomon must have had me in mind when he recorded those words. I was truly blessed when God led me to Thelma. Having her by my side is a blessing that the good Lord gives to me every day–and I thank him for it.

I was twenty-four years old when I met her, and it was love at first sight. We often talk about our first date and how each of us felt as if we had known each other for years. We spent many hours talking and validating our values, ideals, and dreams during our year of courtship before we married. It was a match made in heaven. As Jesus expressed in Matthew 18:18–20: "Truly I tell you, whatever you bind on earth will be bound in heaven, and whatever you loose on earth will be loosed in heaven. Again, truly I tell you, if two of you agree on earth about anything you ask, it will be done for you by my Father in heaven. For when two or three gathered in my name, I am there among them."

Considering the impact on a person's life, undoubtedly the most important decision any of us makes is whom we choose for a mate. One reason why Thelma and I were so right for each other is because we shared a similar spiritual background. Her roots and mine trace back to a youth spent participating in church activities. I believe a spouse who shares your beliefs is the cornerstone of a good marriage.

Before I met Thelma, I didn't truly understand the Scriptures, but as a couple we immersed ourselves in the Word of God, and in time, it became the central theme of our lives. We studied the Bible together, and I gradually began to understand its principles and apply them to our business. Thelma and I prayed at home together–a ritual we practice every morning of our lives. What's more, she prays and sings at home while I am at work. I know it was through her prayer that we were able to overcome our most challenging times. Knowing Thelma is there serves as a mighty source of confidence and reassurance. And what comfort we each receive in knowing that God is always there for us.

When we were first married, we had our share of ups and downs. Over a period of a few years I did some job-hopping, and, in fact, there were two different times when I was unemployed. Once we were living in Los Angeles, and I was working in marketing for the Union Pacific Railroad. I quit that job to move back to St. Louis, thinking I'd land a job in a relatively short time. As things turned out, I didn't have a steady job for about a year, and Thelma worked as a registered nurse to support our family. I brought in some part-time income from my substitute teaching job, but she was our family's main breadwinner. She became a stay-at-home mom after I was hired as a sales rep with Federal Express. I spent a lot of my time on the road being paid a small salary, with bonuses based on making my sales quotas.

A high point of my Federal Express career was being elected into the company's Sales Hall of Fame in 1981. I was one of six honored out of a salesforce of eight hundred. By then, I had become a fairly good salesman, but I sure didn't set the world on fire in the beginning. I had my share of disappointments, and coming home at the end of the day without making a sale is very discouraging. This is when a supportive, loving spouse can be your biggest booster. Thelma never failed to cheer me up after a bad day in the field, making me feel like I would break all sales records the following morning. I've witnessed other sales reps who'd go home to a nagging wife who tore them down for coming home empty-handed after a long day's work. Those reps felt so worn down and discouraged, come morning they could barely drag themselves out the door to their first sales call.

In 1989, a few years after starting my own business, a catastrophe happened that I thought was insurmountable. At the time, I had been so pleased with how well the company was doing and had been waiting for a call from my contact at my biggest account, Union Pacific, to discuss the terms of renewing our contract. Our work with them had been very successful, and I was eagerly anticipating an automatic renewal of the contract. Then a call came from out of the blue–Union Pacific made a decision to drop us. The man explained that everyone was totally satisfied with our auditing services and told me, "You've saved us a bundle, Dave." There was a slight hesitation, and he added: "I'll get right to the point. We have no complaints, and in fact, you did the work so efficiently"–and he paused again–"that we're now in a position to do it internally, so we're not going to renew your contract."

I was so devastated that the only thing I managed to say was,

"I am thankful for the opportunity you gave us to do work for Union Pacific," and hung up the phone.

"What will we do?" I kept asking myself. The Union Pacific account represented 70 percent of our total business. "How will we pay our bills? How can we grow? How can we continue to keep our people on the payroll?"

I needed some cheering up, so I called Thelma to talk, but I didn't have the heart to disappoint her by breaking the news. However, she could tell from the sound of my voice that something was terribly wrong, so I confided in her. She didn't say anything, but that night when I came home, I saw she had prepared one of my favorite meals–fried pork chops, mashed potatoes, and gravy. Sitting there with my wonderful wife and two beautiful children was so inspiring, and I felt so blessed. After dinner, Thelma offered some words of encouragement and said, "Don't worry about it, honey, we'll find a way to make this work." With all that warmth and love in our house, my business problems seemed trivial. I had my loving family and that's what mattered most.

Thelma made sure outside pressures didn't follow me home at the end of the day. Aware of my frustrations, stress from the office, and sheer exhaustion, she made sure our home was a sanctuary, a retreat where I could reenergize and find peace with God. When bill collectors called our house, demanding money that both the business and I owed, Thelma screened those calls, making sure I didn't have to hear what a deadbeat I was. She knew what I was going through at the office and that I didn't need to be hassled at home. One of our favorite songs has a lyric, "You are the wind beneath my wings." Whenever I hear this song, I can't help thinking about Thelma.

Despite the name-calling by bill collectors, my wife never lost faith in me. She has always believed in me and knew I would always do the right thing. She never doubted that my vision for the company would come to fruition. What a remarkable exhibit of belief, considering she doesn't know much about my business. "I don't have to know how your business works," she says lovingly. "I *know* you, and I know God works within you." Thelma's faith in God is strong; she knows he will always provide for her and our children through me.

The Lord has blessed and provided for us beyond what we ever dreamed, so it has been years now since Thelma retired from her nursing job to do volunteer work, the kind of activity that brings her the most pleasure and satisfaction. Thelma has always been active in the community. Even when she was a working mom, she spent time at the church and the children's schools. So community work is nothing new to Thelma, but today, with more time, she is an active board member of many organizations in the St. Louis area. Thelma's constantly chairing events, and as I write this, she is heading a committee for a fund-raiser luncheon, "High Tea," for Girls Inc. I marvel at her high level of energy and enthusiasm, and I am delighted by her commitment to give back to the community. The time and effort she gives to her favorite charities is backed up with financial contributions that we are blessed to be able to make. Sure, Thelma's community work means that she's not at home every night, and I miss having her there, but that's a small price to pay compared to the good deeds she is performing. I love everything about her, and there's not a thing I'd ever want to change.

Finally, a passage from the Bible known as "The Gift of Love," written by Paul, in 1 Corinthians 13:4–7: "Love is patient, love is kind; love is not envious or boastful or arrogant or rude. It does not insist on its own way; it is not irritable or resentful; it does not rejoice in wrongdoing, but rejoices in the truth. It bears all things, believes all things, hopes all things, endures all things." Married people who have this gift of love, as Thelma and I do, are truly blessed by God.

46

ACCOUNTABILITY

If the foot would say, "Because I am not a hand, I do not belong to the body," that would not make it any less a part of the body. And if the ear would say, "Because I am not an eye, I do not belong to the body," that would not make it any less a part of the body. If the whole body were an eye, where would the hearing be? If the whole body were hearing, where would the sense of smell be? But as it is, God arranged the members in the body, each one of them, as he chose. If all were a single member, where would the body be?

—1 Corinthians 12:15–19

If one member suffers, all suffer together with it; if one member is honored, all rejoice together with it.

—1 Corinthians 12:26

The scripture quoted above is referred to as the "One Body with Many Members," or "The Body of Christ." Here, we are told that the body consists of many members, each with its own necessary function that serves other members and the body as a whole. While accountability starts at the top, every member of an organization is held accountable.

Likewise, in every organization, each member contributes to the whole, and every outcome–successful or not so successful–is attributed to all of the members. Each department has its own area of responsibility, and the success of the entire organization depends on the combined performances of all departments. If one member isn't doing what they're supposed to, it affects the whole body. For instance, the sales reps may generate large orders, but what good is that if the plant gets behind in production and can't fulfill orders? Or if the warehouse isn't able to ship units in a timely fashion. Or if the accounting department doesn't send invoices or fails to collect payments due the company! So, like the body, each part depends on all other parts—and each is held accountable for its execution.

A well-run enterprise assigns responsibility to its people along with authority to carry out their assignments. Authority and accountability are like conjoined twins—inseparable. Those with accountability must have enough autonomy to be able to make decisions. There must also be a system in place to measure goals and objectives that have been mutually agreed upon in advance. Without an ongoing method to periodically measure people's performances, no one can be held accountable.

We set up matrices at WWT to assess and measure performance. Several years ago, we invested millions of dollars in Oracle's business system, Enterprise Resource Planning (ERP). This software system is applicable to every aspect of our organization—distribution, warehousing, marketing, sales, operations, customer service. Each aspect of the business is interconnected with every other aspect. ERP is a modern-day version of the lesson taught in the Body of Christ. Here too, each member (that is, vice president, department head, manager, etc.) has a specific function that can be measured to determine how each individual contributes to the entire organization.

The Parable of the Talents (Matthew 25:14–30) also serves as an excellent example of accountability. Here, Jesus tells about a man who entrusted three of his slaves with talents to invest in his absence. When the master returns, he gives more responsibilities to the two slaves who performed well, and he takes away responsibility from the slave who did not. Jesus uses this parable to teach that we are held accountable for our performance–those who perform well are rewarded and given more responsibility, while responsibilities are taken away from poor performers.

The year 2002 will be recorded in history as a time when self-interest and corruption occurred at the highest echelons of some of the nation's largest publicly held companies. Motivated by greed, business leaders misstated corporate financial data to hide losses and exaggerate profits for personal gain. These charlatans traded securities held in their own companies, profiting from inside information unavailable to the public. They put their self-interest ahead of their people's interests or those of their shareholders. They held positions of leadership, but they failed to lead. They could have chosen to be exemplary role models. In their positions in publicly held corporations, they were entrusted to serve their shareholders. In order for the investment industry to function, men and women throughout corporate America must be held accountable. Their illicit deeds did irrefutable harm, eroding the public's trust in our economic system. As a consequence, hundreds of thousands of employees of formerly leading companies such as Enron, Tyco, Global Crossings, Adelphia, WorldCom, and Arthur Andersen (a few of many) lost their jobs. In many instances, their savings in retirement accounts were greatly diminished, if not wiped out altogether. In addition to innocent employees and shareholders incurring personal losses, all Americans were hurt by repercussions that threw the economy into a tailspin. There was an unparalleled loss of faith in the free enterprise system. Granted, only a small percentage of all business leaders were actually guilty; nonetheless, large numbers of innocent people associated with tainted organizations suffered.

Let those self-serving executives who were found guilty and punished serve as an example: Every business leader must be held accountable for his or her actions. As my fellow Missourian Harry Truman often said, "The buck stops here." Business leaders in privately owned companies must also be held accountable–while shareholders might not be involved, these leaders are still obligated to do what's right for their employees, partners, vendors, and other involved parties.

As a CEO, I am the *first* and last person in our organization to be held accountable. This responsibility goes with the title. Every day I set the tone for everyone to follow; my example sets the standard for others to emulate. I do this by following the Word of God and remaining truthful and faithful to the Lord.

Finally, as it is written in Proverbs 29:26, "Many seek the favor of a ruler, but it is from the LORD that one gets justice." Lest we forget, we are not working for man but for the Lord, and it is to him that we are accountable.

47

PRAISE AND RECOGNITION

Do not withhold good from those to whom it is due, when it is in your power to do it.

—Proverbs 3:27

Be generous with your praise and recognition to those who deserve it. And remember: People crave it. Recognition is such a strong motivating force, men risk their lives on the battlefield for ribbons and medals. Athletes spend years in training to win medals in Olympic competition. Actors thrive on applause. Do you remember when Sally Field won the Oscar for her role in *Norma Rae*? How did she react? She exclaimed, "You like me! You really like me!"

Mary Kay Ash, founder of Mary Kay Cosmetics, once referred to the pink Cadillac that her company awards its star salespeople as "a trophy on wheels." She claimed that the monetary value of the award aside, pink Cadillac owners thrived on the recognition they received from onlookers sighting one of these coveted cars parked in a driveway or driving down the road. I have firsthand knowledge of how hard people work to receive recognition. Years ago, when Fred Smith, founder and CEO of Federal Express, presented me with an ice bucket with my name engraved on it at a company banquet, I was on cloud nine. In fact, I still talk about it to this day!

I can vouch that it was the praise and love I received from my mother that drove me to get through college. The same praise and love I received from my wife encouraged me to step out and take that leap of faith to start my own company. Everyone needs support–how well I know–I couldn't have accomplished what I've done by myself. Thelma also gave me a vote of confidence when she made the decision to leave her nursing job and stay home with our two children. Knowing she believed enough in me to know we'd manage without her paycheck was a high form of recognition.

The love and praise I receive at home from my wife, I take with me when I go to work each morning. In John 15:12, when we were told by Jesus to love one another as he loved us, he didn't say anything about limiting our love to our families. He told us to love everyone–all of them.

In Deuteronomy 5:8–10, God commands us not to bow down to or worship idols. He plainly tells us that he is a jealous God, punishing children for the iniquity of parents, to the third and fourth generation of those who reject him. But he rewards unwavering love to the thousandth generation of those who love him and keep his commandments. In this passage, God emphatically tells us that we must recognize him exclusively as God. He demands our praise and recognition. Created in his image, we mortals also seek praise and recognition.

Praise to God is unequaled in relation to what humans merit. Thelma and I often quote something we once heard a minister say, "When praise goes up, blessings come down." Compared to the praise that is due the Lord, certainly we can expect praise only on a minuscule scale. Nonetheless, we respond favorably to what we receive.

1 John 4:4 states that God lives in each and every one of us. This means we must lift up one another and look for ways to give praise when praise is due. Doing this is a tribute to God. It means putting others before ourselves so we may serve them. This is my mission and a focal point of my everyday life.

The highest form of recognition is love. And since God dwells within us, we should love each other. When a person says he loves God but hates his brother or sister, he is not being truthful, because we can't have hateful feelings and correspondingly love God. We praise God by praising his people. And we are reminded in 1 John 4:12 that God lives in us and his love is perfected in us.

Letting people know he cared for them was a trademark of Sam Walton, the late founder and CEO of Wal-Mart. The warm and cozy Walton made people feel comfortable because he made them feel like equals–remarkable for a man, who, if alive today, would be by far the world's richest individual. Throughout his career he donned a baseball cap and made the rounds to his stores in a pickup truck. Walton blended in with everyone. He came across as one of them. "Hey! How's it going?" he'd say as he waved to a customer. He greeted people with a friendly smile, and before long, he was chatting with them about everything from the weather to Little League Baseball. He shared new information with them and sought their opinions about store merchandise, telling them what certain products cost the store and asking what they thought things should sell for. "Thank you. That was a good idea," he'd say on his way out. When he did this, they felt involved and they also felt good about themselves.

If someone waved at you a few years ago in the Wal-Mart parking lot, it might have been Sam.

What does this Waltonism have to do with praise and recognition? The answer is *everything*. Letting people know you care about them and respect them as individuals is a powerful way to express your love for people in business. But to do it right, you must be sincere–otherwise it backfires. I know of a department store chain board chairman who thinks he's emulating Sam Walton when he makes the rounds to a handful of his company's stores every year or two. However, he doesn't drive a pickup. Instead he arrives in a limousine with an entourage of executives, all dressed in dark suits. When they walk into a store, employees don't exactly feel comfortable with his arrival. In fact, they quake and shake. They volunteer little information except for what they think he wants to hear. At the end of the visit, the chairman boasts that he has "walked the walk." He feels good about himself because he "mingled with the troops." What he really liked was that *he* was in the center of attention–it was nothing more than an ego trip. The employees only felt good about the fact that he had left the store and wouldn't be back for a long time.

Unlike Sam Walton, this chairman knows little about engendering feelings of warmth, love, or respect with his people. Instead, he creates an atmosphere of intimidation and resentment. That's because his stroll through the store was all about him, not the employees. This ego trip builds up his self-importance, but to the employees on the floor it is cold and staged. Afterward they resent the way the visit turned out, because it was deceitful. Instead of boosting morale, the chairman's visit had the opposite effect. Your praise and recognition toward others must come from the heart; otherwise it's harmful, not beneficial.

Besides, praise and recognition aren't a matter of making the rounds to see employees and customers on a weekly or monthly basis–it's an everyday activity. Great leaders are constantly in the trenches with their people. They give a lot of praise–deserved praise. They don't praise mediocrity. The high standards of great leaders make those who receive their praise feel special. Their contact is not reserved for high echelon executives. The best leaders go deep into the bowels of their organizations, talking to people at all levels, thanking them for their contribution, letting them know they play a role in the company's success.

Remember: Everyone deserves to be treated with respect, not only a selected few at the top of an organization. The other day, for instance, I was walking through our shipping dock area, and I stopped to shake hands with people loading trucks. I thanked them for working hard for the company. "I know you guys have been here on Saturdays," I said, "and, boy, is that effort making a difference. The customer feedback has been very positive. They really appreciate our expedient delivery–and so do I."

Think about a time when you worked really hard and the exhilarating feeling you had when somebody praised you for it. A good teacher or parent, for example, will praise a young child for doing excellent work, and the child will respond by wanting to excel so he or she can receive more praise. When it comes to receiving praise, we welcome it at all ages. In the workplace, it goes a long way, and I am constantly looking for opportunities to dish it out in large portions when it is deserved. How far does it go in motivating people? Perhaps Mark Twain expressed it best when he said, "I can live for two months on a good compliment."

48

COMPETING TO WIN

The fruit of the Spirit is love, joy, peace, patience, kindness, generosity, faithfulness, gentleness, and self-control. There is no law against such things. And those who belong to Christ Jesus have crucified the flesh with its passions and desires. If we live by the Spirit, let us also be guided by the Spirit. Let us not become conceited, competing against one another, envying one another.

—Galatians 5:22–26

The scripture quoted above represents the fight between righteousness and evil, between the spirit and the flesh, between walking in light or darkness. Each of us has the opportunity to make clear choices. We either allow ourselves to be ruled by greed, or we share with others.

To some people, competing means winning at any cost. "It's a dog-eat-dog world out there," they say. "You learn to swim with the sharks or you'll get eaten alive." They discredit what Jesus told us in Luke 6:27–29: that we should love our enemy, turn the other cheek, and that if anyone takes away our shirt, we should give our shirt to him. To them, turning the other cheek is just an invitation for a hard slap in the face.

They don't subscribe to the philosophy that the meek shall inherit the earth (Matthew 5:5). To their way of thinking, when it comes to business, giving and caring are weaknesses. These qualities seem to them diametrically opposed to what it takes to climb the corporate ladder. They believe rising to the top echelon of an organization is achieved by shoving, kicking, and clawing. They let it be known that anyone who gets in their way will be run over.

These people are under the erroneous opinion that anyone who follows the ways of Jesus is neither strong nor aggressive. Boy, do they underestimate what I think is their *real* competition. They fail to realize that business success isn't based on knocking down the other guy or attacking the vulnerable. On the contrary, a strong competitor wins by continually doing what is best for employees and customers, always placing their interest above his or her own. Loyalty is won by outperforming the competition, not by steamrolling it.

Rather than entertain negative thoughts about your competition, focus on positive thoughts about what you can do to benefit others. This will help build long-term relationships. True, it might take you a while longer to prove yourself to the customer, because you don't wow people with pie-in-the-sky promises that you can't keep. On the contrary, you win by understating your promises and regularly overdelivering services rendered. In the long run, you'll win their respect and lasting loyalty. Wait until those cutthroat competitors try to steal your customers–this is when they find out your so-called "weaknesses" were actually strengths.

At times, I've gone head-on against a competitor who played by a different set of rules than I. I recall a particular situation when my company was struggling to survive. Several companies had put in bids to a large prospect, which had narrowed its choice to one other competitor and us. To get the account, the other company made unrealistic promises we knew they couldn't fulfill. I don't believe in knocking the competition, so we remained silent, hoping the prospect would realize the truth and we'd get the business. It didn't, and we didn't get the account. At the time, it was disappointing because we knew we'd do a better job.

When I first started our company, I knew there would be many disappointments–that's business. I was well aware things wouldn't always go our way. These were the times when it helped to remember a verse in Isaiah 41:10 that told me not to fear and to know that God was with us, and he would make us strong. Believing this was a source of enormous reinforcement, my faith in the Lord assured me that with him by our side, we would hold our own against all competition.

For years, we had competed head-on against Dell Computers, a giant and a highly respected company in the direct-selling computer industry. I didn't want to compete with Dell, because I saw an advantage for both sides if we became partners; each of us had certain strengths that complemented each other. But Dell didn't see it that way, so we remained competitors. In time, however, they began to hear our customers say good things about us. After enough people pointed out our strengths, Dell decided to meet with us. As a result, Dell realized the advantages of working with us, and we have developed a wonderful partnership. Today, we're one of their biggest partners, a win-win situation for both companies.

Speaking of win-win situations, there's a story going around about a hundred-yard dash that recently took place at the Seattle Special Olympics. When the gun went off to start the race, one young runner stumbled and hurt his knee. When the other eight children heard him cry, they stopped running and went back to help him–all of them. A little girl with Down's syndrome planted a kiss on his forehead and said, "This will make it better." The little boy stood up and the nine children linked their arms together and happily walked to the finish line. There was a long, roaring standing ovation in the stadium–and not a dry eye. These special children taught everyone in the stands a good lesson that day. Winning isn't only about who finishes first–it's about helping others to win too.

Remember that employees and customers make choices. Employees select which companies to work for, customers select those deserving of their business, and so on. What kind of employers do you think inspire workers to be more productive and loyal? An employer who uses browbeating and intimidating tactics to drive people? Or an employer who is concerned about their welfare and treats them with respect? Likewise, which kind of company do you think builds long-term relationships with customers? A company that negotiates contracts designed to squeeze the last nickel out of them and provide the least possible service? Or a company devoted to maximizing value and providing above-and-beyond-the-call-of-duty service? When you think about it and make these comparisons, you wonder how any businessperson could fail to grasp the principles of the Bible as an excellent guide to conduct business.

IMPLEMENTATION

Be doers of the world, and not merely hearers who deceive themselves.

—James 1:22

This scripture advises us not just to contemplate our visions of grandeur, but to carry out our ambitious intentions. A Fortune 500 CEO once said to me, "There is no shortage of an abundance of good ideas coming across my desk. If I had a nickel for every good idea I've heard, I could retire." It is not the want of good ideas that handicaps an organization, but the failure to implement them.

A team effort is required to assure success, but it takes the leadership of a single person to make a team jell. This individual focuses on a specific goal and has passion and a willingness to take charge. Leading by example, this person is a catalyst whose enthusiasm energizes and motivates other team members. The leader's faith that the project will succeed becomes contagious, and soon, everyone buys into it.

The leader's faith inspires others to share the vision–and to also believe it will happen. However, heed what we are told in James 2:17: "Faith by itself, if it has no works, is dead." So while having faith is a necessary ingredient, it takes more than belief to make things happen. Strong faith provides an impetus, but that faith must intermesh with hard work; otherwise, you've got only a pipe dream.

In our organization, when a good idea is presented and approved, we don't stand idly by, procrastinating, pondering what to do about it. Once the decision has been made to move forward, management gets behind it with our full support. This means providing necessary resources for its fulfillment. We put our money where our mouth is. The project receives the best tools, training, education, and whatever else it takes to demonstrate our support. I believe management must demonstrate its seriousness by making an investment. Hedging and withholding on funding signifies lack of confidence in the project.

Implementation requires accepting change. In the fast-paced world of technology, a company must be light on its feet and capable of change–if not, its success is doubtful. Consequently, at WWT we embrace change and commonly have kickoff events to launch a new project. One such event took place when we introduced our Enterprise Resource Planning System (ERP), a program that affected every aspect of our business. ERP necessitated reengineering the entire organization and, at the same time, we had to keep the company running while ERP was in the process of being implemented–a huge undertaking. This prompted us to launch ERP with a major kickoff to start the ball rolling. We wanted everyone to focus on ERP as a companywide top priority. To keep everyone current, we set up planning information teams to educate everyone on how ERP works. To capture our people's attention, we put on skits involving people at all levels, to the top echelons of the company. Not only were these skits a lot of fun, they demonstrated the support and passion we all have for ERP.

Being a technology company, we have built-in awareness of

the importance of implementation that not all companies have. We've seen other companies invest heavily in software but lack the know-how to integrate it into their business. The technology they buy brings no value if no one in the company knows how to use it effectively. Without implementation, systems add no real value. Likewise, technicians who don't clearly understand the business will be unable to devise systems relevant to solving problems.

Then there are those corporate executives who refuse to make a business decision without conferring with their legal people for approval. While legal opinions can be valuable feedback and an important piece of the equation for the decision-making process, there's no question that the legalese input a lawyer brings to the table can squelch an otherwise doable business deal. All too often, lawyers look for reasons why a deal won't work. The same applies to accountants–while we need their counseling, as well as that of attorneys, a business decision should be based on the merits of the business deal, not legal and accounting technicalities. If a deal makes good sense and has sound business merit, attorneys and accountants can be brought in as support people to advise how to make the deal work. Of course, we must rely on lawyers to write required legal documents and accountants to review the numbers. Personally, I prefer to do business on a handshake, based on the relationship I have with people. I rely heavily on what that little voice inside me says I should do. It's a matter of doing business with people you trust, knowing they will stand by their word.

Many good ideas never get implemented because they get bogged down in committees. Committees that aren't properly run stifle implementation. Projects get tabled for further discussion to be considered at future committee meetings. In time, good ideas are dropped for the next "flavor-of-the-week" idea. For this reason, I offer the following ten suggestions for committee meetings:

1. **To assure a productive meeting, have a clear, stated purpose that all participants know and understand.**
2. **Circulate an agenda before the meeting. It should be limited to items pertaining to the meeting's purpose.**
3. **Advise participants to come prepared. This means they do their homework in advance.**
4. **Include only those individuals who will contribute. Consider inviting only those who have a vested interest in its outcome.**
5. **Limit the meeting to a specific length of time, say, one hour maximum.**
6. **Stick to your agenda.**
7. **Review progress reports of implementation so results can be evaluated.**
8. **At its end, summarize the meeting, mentioning what has been decided, what action will be taken, and who is responsible to do it.**
9. **Schedule the next meeting to monitor results and make additional assignments.**
10. **Communicate, communicate, communicate.**

In addition to the ten suggestions above, a successful meeting must have focus. The implementation of any project requires a clear definition of the mission. If people go in circuitous directions, the waste of time and energy will create confusion and distraction. As Jesus reminds us in Matthew 6:24, we can't serve two masters. This is excellent advice in business. Small entrepreneurs who fail to heed these words move in all directions, trying to cater to all customers and, in the process, become unable to effectively serve anyone. You'll find this also in large corporations. At one time, Sears was the world's largest retailer. Its slogan was: "Sears has everything." Even the then-mighty Sears discovered it couldn't have everything for everyone.

50

THE JOY OF GIVING

. . . to whom much has been given, much will be required.

—Luke 12:48

It often happened before I went to Sunday school as a young boy. On my way out the door, my mother would frantically search through the kitchen cupboard and her purse looking for money. Finally she'd pull out an old wrinkled dollar bill or some change from her red jar, and putting it in my small hand, she'd say, "Honey, we're down to our last dollar. When they pass the collection plate around, be sure to put this in it, because we need some money."

I knew we needed money but didn't know we were poor, and I truly believe there were times I gave away our last dollar. However, giving the money away made my mother believe something supernatural would happen. Her faith strengthened mine, as it taught me the joy of giving. I saw that my mother, in giving away that last dollar, received so much more than from anything she could have bought with it.

Each time I read a parable told by Jesus in Luke 21:1–4, I think about my mother. Here, he compares a poor widow's contribution of two small copper coins to the charitable gifts of rich people. To paraphrase Jesus, a destitute person who gives what he or she must live on is more generous than wealthy people whose contributions do not alter their affluent lifestyle. Some of the most charitable people on this earth are those dedicated men and women across America who collectively volunteer millions of hours of their time to their churches and local communities. Yes, they give their money. But those selfless hours they spend on bake sales, collecting and recycling old clothes, and conducting Bible study classes represent the spirit behind their giving. My firsthand knowledge of this first came from seeing my mother volunteering her time even while she ran a household of eight needy children, always finding time to be a volunteer in the Boy Scouts, Campfire Girls, and the PTA. Today I see my wife, Thelma, active in our church and serving on several community boards.

Another lesson that my mother taught us about giving is the way she never let a hobo who came to our door go away hungry. And because we lived right next to the railroad tracks, hobos stopped by frequently for a free meal. Whenever one came to our door, she'd always take food from our refrigerator and serve him on the front porch. Years later, I found out that a painted sign on a power pole in front of our property let them know they were welcome at the Steward home.

Although a good portion of my time is spent traveling across the country on business trips, I set aside time to serve my community. I am currently a board member of fourteen charitable and civic organizations. I am a board director of United Way of St. Louis, Boy Scouts of America, Toys for Tots, Barnes Jewish Hospital, Webster University, Ronald McDonald House, Inroads, the Benevolent Society Association, Regional Commerce Growth Association, and Civic Progress, to name a few. Civic Progress is an organization consisting of members of the area's largest companies; its mission is guiding and supporting the community and its various charitable groups. I'm slated to serve as the board chairman of United Way of St. Louis in 2006. Our United Way unit is ranked as one of the top in the United States; in 2002, it raised in excess of $67 million.

I am frequently asked to serve on corporate boards of publicly held companies, but so far I've turned them all down. "You can average $50,000 in fees per corporate board," one friend advised me, "and you can also get valuable stock options." Another friend says his own annual director's fees exceed $250,000 from four corporate boards. If it was a matter of money, I wouldn't be on any boards, because focusing on my own business is the best use of my time. But it's not about the money. Giving my time and money to the community is a part of my life that I cherish. As Jesus teaches in Luke 12:48: *"to whom much has been given, much will be required."* For the past nine years, I have tithed, as the Bible teaches us, which means a minimum of 10 percent of my personal income goes to charity.

Personal giving aside, my company strives to be a good corporate citizen. We exist to serve our employees, customers, vendors, partners, *and* the community. On this subject, I believe every business is obligated to give back to the community. It's a two-way street. The schools contribute to the welfare of its local companies by providing good educations to its children. Let's keep in mind that the boys and girls in our schools represent a large pool of future talent in the local workforce. Then too, I consider institutions such as the art museum, symphony, opera, and professional sports teams as valuable community assets. That's because they attract employees and customers to live in the St. Louis area. Likewise, excellent hospitals, strong police protection, and colleges benefit a city's general public and hence, its home-based companies. A viable community provides real value to our company. While our reason for giving is not focused on receiving, it's obvious that good corporate citizens really do receive in return, though not necessarily from those whom they serve.

A 2002 survey taken by America's Research Group revealed convincing statistical evidence that being a good corporate citizen enhances a company's bottom line. The ARG study disclosed the following:

- **63 percent of Americans stated they would purchase more goods and services from a company active in its community than with one that was not.**
- **62 percent rated a company's charity involvement as an important factor in choosing where to make a purchase.**
- **78 percent of the interviewees trust a company that is active in the community.**
- **81 percent claimed it made them feel more loyal.**
- **83 percent say it's something they talk about with their friends and family.**
- **95 percent boasted that their bosses' civic activities made them feel proud about working for the company.**

At WWT, our giving has no strings attached, but the above survey illustrates that being a good corporate citizen generates strong employee and customer loyalty, and is good for the bottom line. If profits are enhanced, that's just a bonus. We give because it's the right thing to do. Besides, giving is deeply ingrained in our culture. Our giving spirit toward employees, customers, vendors, and partners extends to the entire community. We apply the "Love one another as I have loved you" teaching of Jesus to our everyday activities—true giving has no boundaries. Our community involvement sets a tone internally for the entire company. We have no ulterior motives, and this, I believe, establishes a level of trust that permeates every aspect of our organization. And when we give, we give with joy. As 2 Corinthians 9:7 reminds us, God loves a cheerful giver.

While we give cheerfully, we do make decisions regarding what we support. Like every responsible company, we have budgets. For this reason, it isn't possible for us to make contributions to every solicitation we receive, no matter how worthy the cause. The United Way is the single biggest recipient of our company's charitable contributions. We give generously to the United Way because it supports over two hundred other agencies in the St. Louis area that, in turn, touch one out of three people in our community. We encourage our employees to give to United Way but, of course, it's voluntary. Many have favorite charities of their own they support. Still, an estimated 60 to 70 percent of our employees contribute to the annual United Way drive.

As a company, we focus our attention on supporting organizations that cater to needy families and children. Why? Because children represent the next generation, and we want these young people to have a sense of hope. Two of these organizations are Toys for Tots and Ronald McDonald House. We usually sponsor a golf tournament for the latter that raises about $100,000 a year. To make fund-raising fun at WWT, we conduct many raffles throughout the year that include prizes donated by some of our vendors. The company owns luxury suites for professional football, baseball, basketball, and hockey events. These boxes have twelve to sixteen seats, and when you add up the total number of games in all seasons, they accommodate a lot of people throughout the year. We use them to entertain our customers, vendors, and employees and we also donate use of the suites to be raffled off in various fund-raising events to generate revenue for worthy causes. For instance, we recently auctioned the baseball suite for a night game, with proceeds going to The Girls, Inc. Another time, it went to the highest bidder for a United Way fund-raiser. When a customer or vendor cancels, making some extra seats in a box available, we give them to local groups that bring young boys and girls who may not otherwise have an opportunity to see a professional sports event. We make sure a catering service keeps our suites well stocked with food and soft drinks for our guests.

We encourage our employees to support charitable and civic organizations, and whatever they give, the company matches with an equal amount to the same charity. There is no limit to how much we match–dollar for dollar, we match 100 percent. Employees appreciate the fact that WWT supports what *they* support.

One of my favorite times is when schoolchildren visit our premises. Groups of thirty-five to forty boys and girls come here throughout the year. In addition to taking a tour of our operations, students attend a presentation on business career opportunities in America, and depending on the time of day, we provide lunch or snacks. Some of these children from the inner city have had little contact with businesspeople, except perhaps the mom-and-pop stores in their neighborhood. Here, they see something different, and hopefully they recognize it as a promising option. During the presentation, I speak to them about my personal experiences, including growing up in the small town of Clinton, Missouri. I'm candid with them about my struggles to maintain a C average in high school, and I stress the importance of getting a good education. "I was only an average student. You can do better than I did," I say. "Many people thought I'd never go to college, especially as a business major, and some felt that if I did, I'd never graduate. But I did. So remember that no matter what other people think, it's *what you know you can do that counts.* And always remember that God is with you."

The boys and girls who visit us range in age from eight years old to college students. One day, a group of inner-city kids may visit, and the next, an Inroads group. Inroads is a wonderful organization that helps college students who have maintained a good grade-point average. It provides them with job opportunities during the summer months, in addition to training and developing them for their post-grad careers. In December, we invite Toys for Tots to visit us. This group provides toys to children of parents whose resources are low. Two years ago, we hosted over a thousand kids throughout the Christmas holidays and had toys for every one of them. On one of those days, Michael Jones, the St. Louis Rams player who made the game-saving tackle in the Super Bowl XXXIV game between the St. Louis Rams and Nashville Titans, visited the office. Jones, who is an excellent speaker, joined me on the podium to talk to the kids.

The following Christmas, each of the buildings on our company campus competed to collect the most toys for Toys for Tots. Our employees provided toys, plus they brought in toys solicited from their friends and neighbors as well as from our vendors and customers. The toys were put on display in each building lobby, mostly gift-wrapped. In total, we had several thousand toys to give away to the children who visited us during the holiday season. Kurt Warner, the Rams star quarterback, his wife, Brenda, and two of their children stopped in for a few hours while a group of kids was here. At the end of the day, the children stood in line to receive an autographed Bible from him.

51

LET GO AND LET GOD

For it is God who is at work in you, enabling you both to will and to work for his good pleasure.

—Philippians 2:13

I have always trusted in the Lord, knowing that he is there for me. I never doubt he will look over me, and he always does. It's interesting because sometimes God's blessings come to us in unexpected ways. For example, in 1993, a WWT team was working overtime to land a multimillion dollar contract with the air force. At the time, this single deal would have tripled our $17 million company. We were having major cash-flow problems, and we badly needed this business.

Over a period of six months, we invested thousands of hours in our pursuit to close this deal; our out-of-pocket expenses were approximately $150,000, which was a lot of money to the company. We worked very hard to win the contract and were confident we'd beat the other four companies also competing for the job. Finally, the air force narrowed it down to another competitor and us, and they asked for our final bids. We were elated and told ourselves we'd soon reap the rewards for all the time and effort we put into this project. The other company, however, ended up winning the job, and it appeared all our hard work was for naught. We were down in the dumps, scratching our heads trying to figure out what to do next.

Then, we were blessed when the General Services Administration (GSA) contacted us and said it was looking for a company with technology expertise to assist it in a new start-up program. Although we were small, the GSA had heard good things about us from some of our customers. WWT's current president, Joe Koenig, who at the time was our vice president of sales and marketing, accompanied me to the initial meeting with the GSA in Washington, D.C. When we saw its interest, we envisioned our company as a viable candidate for its business, and we focused all of our energies on winning the contract. At the time, our cash flow was so tight, our survival was on the line. Miraculously, within sixty days, we had a deal signed, sealed, and delivered with the GSA. After the contract, our annual sales of $17 million zoomed to $74 million. This contract was much bigger than the one we worked so hard to get with the air force. Our two previous contracts with the federal government had been considerably smaller. The GSA contract established us as a real player with the government. It was the catalyst that created efficiencies within our company that enabled us to expand our business on a much larger scale. The GSA contract was exceptionally successful, and it distinguished WWT as a leader in our industry, evidenced by awards we received as a result of this work.

The GSA contract springboarded our company into becoming a competitive government supplier. It also helped us expand into additional nongovernmental areas. A miraculous thing about this contract is that it generally takes six months to a year from the time we have an initial contact with a government agency until it's closed. This contract took only sixty days from start to finish. I'm not sure we could have stayed in business if we'd had to wait a full year. Whenever I'm asked to explain what we did, I can only reply, "It came from God."

Sometimes people shake their head in doubt when I credit God for the good fortune I have enjoyed. It's as if they want to hear a secret, complex explanation rather than believe that prayer works. I know prayer works, and I frequently pray to God while I'm at work. When I'm talking business on the telephone, at times I excuse myself for a minute or two to pray for guidance.

They say there are no atheists in foxholes. People sometimes experience a quick spurt of faith in dire times. Later, when the danger has passed, they may drop their faith, as if they no longer need it. Still other people have faith in God when they start out in business, but once they succeed, they forget how they got there. They start talking about what great things they did–not what God did for them. This is one reason Thelma and I conduct the Doing Business by the Good Book Sunday school classes. We want to let people know that God is the reason we are where we are today. We tell them they can do what we did–believe in the Word of God, and stand fast on it. Let's always remember what Paul writes in Philippians 4:13: "I can do all things through him (Christ Jesus) who strengthens me."

When we were still in our infancy, we believed we would someday be a billion-dollar company. Today, as a billion-dollar company, we say we will someday be a $10 billion company. It won't happen until you say it and believe it. In John 20:29, Jesus asks the question: "Have you believed because you have seen me?" He then adds, "Blessed are those who have not seen and yet have come to believe." This wonderful thought directs us toward realizing our $10 billion dream. It starts with faith. Then we let go and let God.

52

GOD BLESS AMERICA

But I have said to you: You shall inherit their land, and I will give it to you to possess, a land flowing with milk and honey. I am the LORD your God; I have separated you from the peoples.

—Leviticus 20:24

In the above verse, God spoke of the Promised Land across the Jordan that awaited the Israelites, who, at the time, were wandering in the wilderness. I view America as today's Promised Land. Of the more than 6 billion people in this world, only 280 million–less than 5 percent of the world's population–are Americans. While we live in a land of plenty, sadly, billions of men, women, and children around the globe will go to bed hungry this very night.

To live in America is a blessing from God. Our land is indeed rich and fertile; it has vast resources. Yet our abundant farmlands and great industry are not our greatest assets. There are other nations endowed with bounteous resources, but our prosperity dwarfs any other. The Constitution handed down to us by our forefathers upholds the sanctity of the individual. Our great heritage has produced a culture that empowers its citizens without regard to religion, race, or background. We have evolved into a nation with unrivaled economic and military power.

Throughout the course of civilization, no nation has ever given so much to other nations. No nation has ever held such a stalwart leadership role. America's compassion to other countries was evidenced following World War II, when billions of U.S. dollars were spent through the Marshall Plan rebuilding Europe and Japan.

Early settlers, high-spirited and daring, came to America to pioneer a vast, virgin land. These brave men and women encountered famine and disease; still their spirit remained unbroken. Through valleys of huge mountain ranges, they pushed westward into an unknown land, not knowing what lay on the other side. The farms and ranches they settled on were often miles away from the nearest neighbor. Isolated, they were profoundly independent. These early settlers epitomize today's American spirit, a heritage passed down to us.

The patriots of the first thirteen colonies, protesting taxation without representation, sought sovereignty and freedom from the British. Signing the Declaration of Independence was the same as declaring war on England, at the time the most powerful nation in the world–comparable today to tiny Costa Rica waging war against the United States. The signers of the Declaration of Independence were willing to risk their lives for their beliefs. They affixed their signatures to a doctrine that declared: "We hold these truths to be self-evident that all men are created equal, they are endowed by their creator with certain inalienable rights. That among these are life, liberty and the pursuit of happiness." Think about it–this unparalleled document declares that every American citizen has the right to pursue happiness. Only in America are citizens given this inalienable right.

Note too that this document reveres God, as does our Constitution and our Pledge of Allegiance. Look in your wallet: All this nation's paper currency is inscribed, "In God we trust." Our nation's chief executive officers have traditionally made reference to God. The following are a few quotations from past presidents:

> Direct my thought, words and work, wash away my sins in the immaculate Blood of the Lamb, and purge my heart by Thy Holy Spirit. . . . Daily frame me more and more into the likeness of Thy Son Jesus Christ.
>
> —George Washington, First President

> With a good conscience our only sure reward, with history the final judge of our deeds, let us go forth to lead the land we love, asking His blessing and His help, but knowing that from here on, God's work must truly be our own.
>
> —John F. Kennedy, Thirty-fifth President

> The Lord our God be with us, as He was with our fathers; may He not leave us or forsake us; so that we may incline our hearts to Him, to walk in all His ways . . . that all peoples of the earth may know that the Lord is God; there is no other.
>
> —George H. W. Bush, Forty-first President

As our leaders prayed that God would direct them to do the right thing for our nation, and regardless of our political party, we should support the president who is in office, praying for him or her to receive wisdom from above. Decisions made in the Oval Office affect each and every one of us, determining how we work and how our families live.

Evil leaders rule only a handful of nations; our focus must be on the greater good that the United States of America represents. The anti-American rhetoric around the world is fostered by hateful leaders who, sadly, have aimed a torrent of hate at our country. Their rhetoric is an attempt to cover up their governments' failure to deliver liberty and opportunity to their own people. This ill will toward America surfaced in the despicable acts of terrorism committed against humankind on September 11, 2001. Despite the enormous tragedy, the resiliency of a united American people demonstrated our will to overcome evil.

One of America's unique strengths is the large number of people who have migrated to this country. It started with early colonists who sought religious freedom. The first big flood of 13.5 million immigrants arrived at our shores between 1860 and 1900—Germans, Irish, Italians, Lithuanians, Poles, Russians, Swedes. This mass migration firmly established America as the melting pot of the world. In more recent years, immigrants came from Mexico and Central America, the Pacific Rim, the Middle East. And over 30 million African-Americans have roots tracing back to Africa. Then, of course, consider the Native Americans. We are all members of this splendid melting pot. I believe this diversity is behind America's greatness. We are unquestionably the most ethnically diverse people in the world. What is the glue that holds us all together? It is our patriotism and our allegiance to the ideal that we are one nation under God.

Millions have come to America to live in a land of freedom and opportunity; they got what they came for. Where else but in America could I have come from an underprivileged family in a small, rural town and encountered so much opportunity? Ragsto-riches stories in other countries are rare compared to the United States. My story is only one of millions in America. I feel blessed to live in this great country, and I can think of no more appropriate way to conclude this book than by saying, *God bless America* . . . now let Americans bless God.